GRAND SLAM
ENGLAND IN AUSTRALIA 1986/87

GRAND SLAM
ENGLAND IN AUSTRALIA 1986/87
A CRICKETER SPECIAL

Christopher Martin-Jenkins
Photographs by Adrian Murrell
Statistics by Richard Lockwood

SIMON SCHUSTER

First published in Great Britain by
Simon & Schuster Limited 1987

Simon & Schuster Limited, West Garden Place,
Kendal Street, London W2 2AQ

Simon & Schuster Australia Pty Limited

British Library Cataloguing in Publication Data

Martin-Jenkins, Christopher
Grand Slam: England in Australia 1986/87:
a cricketer special
1. Cricket – Australia. 2. Cricket – England
I. Title
796.35'865 GV928.A8
ISBN 0 671 65512 4

Made by Lennard Books Ltd, Windmill Cottage,
Mackerye End, Harpenden, Herts AL5 5DR
Editor Michael Leitch
Designed by Pocknell & Co
Printed and bound in Great Britain
by Butler & Tanner Ltd, Frome and London

Errata

Please note the following corrections to
caption directions

page 55	(top) and (above) should be transposed
page 64	(below) should refer to Gus Logie
page 103	(left) and (right) should be transposed

CONTENTS

CHAPTER ONE

BACKGROUND TO A TRIUMPH

Eleven Tests played; eight lost; three drawn. It had been for the England cricket team of 1986 as bleak a period as any since 1921 when, in a mere eight months, Warwick Armstrong's Australia had savaged England under the captaincy of J.W.H.T. Douglas, winning the first eight Tests after the Great War.

It took unusual percipience to predict that in 1986–87 England would belie their recent form as confidently and comprehensively as they did under Mike Gatting in Australia. Yet there *was* evidence that England's carefully selected team had a real opportunity of success, even though few had enough optimism to see it. The most significant pointer was that England's previous series against Australia, at home in 1985, had resulted in a most clear-cut victory, marked by unusual, indeed almost unprecedented domination of the Australian bowling. England's batsmen averaged an extraordinary 60 runs per 100 balls over the whole series, rattling up totals of 533 in the first Test, 456 in the third, 482 for nine in the fourth and 595 for five in the fifth. Only at Lord's did they fail to make a first-innings score in excess of 300, and they duly lost that match. England won the series, however, by three matches to one, based upon bold and attractive batting by Tim Robinson and the three Gs, Gower, Gatting and Gooch. Good pitches and weak Australian bowling also explained their triumph.

But, a year later, what a contrast! David Gower had lost his job as captain to Mike Gatting, who, though he had played with success in Grade cricket in Australia, had never been there on an official tour.

Tim Robinson had lost his place in the side. Graham Gooch had decided not to tour. England had lost 0–5 to the West Indies – for the second time in 18 months – and then, less explicably, had lost at home to India and also, for the first time on home soil, to New Zealand.

At the start of the 1986 season in England one would have guessed that England's true ability lay somewhere about halfway between the disaster in the Caribbean and the 1985 triumph against Australia. But the home defeats at the hands of two countries whose welcome presence in England had nevertheless often in the past been viewed with a rather patronizing air by all concerned with English cricket, came as an unpleasant surprise. A Committee of Inquiry under Charles Palmer had already reported on the problems facing English cricket but, in the true tradition of such official inquiries, its recommendations had largely been ignored, partly because of a renewed complacency arising from the 1985 success against Australia.

There *were* things which needed correcting in English cricket, without doubt, ranging from the decline of the game in many schools to England's complicity in the general over-indulgence in international cricket generally. But my own view was that the defeats by India and New Zealand in 1986 looked much worse than they were, for four main reasons. Firstly, the cruel defeat imposed on them in the Caribbean earlier in the year had resulted in a collective loss of confidence and form which both India and New Zealand were admirably able to exploit. The batsmen, especially, were literally and metaphorically on the back foot, looking still for the short ball which would explode in their faces like the one which had broken Mike Gatting's nose at Sabina Park.

Secondly, there had been a change of leader, with Gatting taking over from David Gower, somewhat reluctantly at first, and taking time to believe in his own ability to do the job.

Thirdly, England had been without Ian Botham until the last Test of the summer, due to a ban imposed on him after an admission of drug-taking. But his presence in the last Test of the summer seemed to have a revivifying effect on all around him. He took a wicket with his first ball back in Test cricket and then produced one of those unique bursts of hitting which enable him to bat like a blacksmith in a Test match and make world-class bowlers look like tired trundlers from Tillingford-under-Lyme.

Finally, bleak season though it was, England did, in fact, twice get into positions from which they might have won, only to be interrupted by the weather. At Edgbaston in July India had been 131 for five, needing 236, with 24 overs still left and Edmonds on the rampage. And at the Oval against New Zealand, England had responded to New Zealand's 287 on a good wicket with 388 for five at a helter-skelter rate which had sounded distinct echoes from the summer before, not least because Gatting and Gower made centuries.

A form-guide to the next Ashes series was easily available, since India and New Zealand had, as it happened, been the guests in Australia the previous winter when India had had much the better of a drawn series and New Zealand had won easily, the redoubtable Richard Hadlee to the fore. Therefore, most were drawn to the embarrassing conclusion that on current form the two founder members of

Test cricket were the weakest teams. In fact, however, there was little to choose between any of the nations standing in the queue behind the West Indies who, despite occasional frailties in their batting and an almost total reliance on fast bowlers which made them vulnerable on the rare occasions that they met out-and-out spinning conditions, were still certain to beat any of the other countries over a five-match rubber.

Australia, moreover, appeared to be turning the corner after a run at least as barren as England's. They toured India in September and October as part of their preparation for the visit of England. It was a moot point whether they should have done so in view of the exceptionally heavy season of international cricket which faced them at home, but at least it gave Allan Border and his team a chance to build on the slight improvement they had begun to show on a tour of New Zealand at the end of the previous Australian season. (For Border himself there had been no respite in between since he had undertaken almost a full season for Essex. It was hardly surprising that after the unexpected reverse he and his team were to suffer in the first Test at Brisbane his temper snapped and, not for the first time, he came close to resigning his daunting commission.)

In India, the young Australian side certainly did make some progress. The Test in Madras reached as pulsating a climax as any in the history of the game. Australia made most of the running, with Dean Jones scoring a double century in extreme heat and humidity which turned him overnight from a brilliantly talented but impetuous young batsman into a genuine Test player capable of truly exceptional deeds. Border then declared their second innings, dangling a carrot in the best traditions of the game. The upshot was only the second tied match in Test history as Greg Matthews won an lbw appeal against Maninder Singh with the scores level. Rain spoiled the drawn match in Delhi but at Bombay Australia showed character to bat themselves out of trouble after being 172 behind on first innings. It was clear enough that in Marsh, Boon, Jones, Border, Ritchie, Matthews and Waugh they had now established a solid batting platform.

To all who looked closely at the evidence of their last few seasons, however, it was equally clear that the Australians, having lost several of the best contenders to the team unofficially representing their country in South Africa, were desperately short of bowlers of genuine Test class. Craig McDermott, so promising in 1985, had lost his way, and although Bruce Reid, six foot eight inches, left-arm over with an exceptionally rhythmic action for one of his gangling build, had established himself the previous year, he had a miserable time in India taking one wicket at a cost of 222 in the Tests. (Mind you, this was one more than Dennis Lillee once managed on a tour of Pakistan; the pitches of the Sub-Continent are not the sort of which fast bowlers dream, except when their sleep is very disturbed.) Greg Matthews, who had not bothered many English batsmen in 1985, had easily the best Test figures of 14 for 407 in the three matches. Ray Bright, who in several appearances at home and away against England had made little impression, also did well, taking eight wickets at 36 apiece in the three high-scoring Tests.

What also stood out when the English and Australian teams were compared, in the early weeks of the tour, was the gap in experience. This fact was clouded by England's early batting failures – of which more anon – but whereas England had Gower, with 86 caps, Botham with 85, Gatting with 48, Lamb with 46,

Edmonds with 41 and Emburey, newly appointed vice-captain, with 37, Border stood out alone for Australia with 81 previous games. None of the other certain selections had played more than 20 games. Geoff Lawson, whose fitness was in doubt, had 36 caps, Bright 22, Wayne Phillips, thought to be out of favour with manager Bobby Simpson, 27, and Greg Ritchie 23. By the end of the season the nations's vice-captain would be a man who had started the series with experience of only nine Tests: the tough, self-made opener from Wandering, 'Swampy' Marsh.

Around their experienced nucleus Peter May and his England Selection Committee had gathered a well-balanced combination. Their most crucial decision, as time would tell, was to reinstate a man who had been most harshly discarded two years before. Chris Broad had averaged 31 in five Tests in 1984, four of them against the West Indies at their furious best, yet had been overlooked for the subsequent tour of India. His courage and sound technique had deserved a better reward than this and he must have viewed with a mixture of pleasure and mortification the rise and fall of his county opening partner Tim Robinson who, after scoring 934 runs at an average of 62 in his first year in Test cricket (against India and Australia) then failed so badly against the West Indies that he was dropped after one home Test against India in 1986.

Personally I would have found a place for Robinson in the touring party of 16 and it will be a surprise if he does not again perform with distinction for England. The one real surprise in the official choice, however, was the inclusion of Wilf Slack of Middlesex, who won a place ahead of several other aspiring opening batsmen, including Martyn Moxon, Robert Bailey (not a specialist opener) and Ashley Metcalfe. Even so, seven specialist batsmen were picked, young James Whitaker being the nearest thing to a gamble, though his brilliant season for Leicestershire had earned him a chance ahead of candidates who included two highly, almost equally successful men from the North, John Morris and Neil Fairbrother.

It looked to me at the time as though the Selectors had erred in picking one too many batsmen and one too few all-rounders. In the event both Slack and Whitaker took virtually no part in the later proceedings of the tour and an extra all-rounder – my choice would have been David Capel of Northants – would have been extremely handy at that stage as the regular members of the 'first team' grew stale and weary through the long series of limited-overs internationals.

As for the bowlers, the Selectors only chose those whom most of the pundits had predicted and recommended: Dilley, Foster, Small and the exciting 20-year-old Phillip DeFreitas, who had taken 94 wickets at 23 in his first full season. They were to prove the correct choices to bowl fast – hard though this was on Richard Ellison, a hero when England had played Australia in 1985, on Greg Thomas, who had done quite well on his demanding first tour of the West Indies, and on Derek Pringle, who had not let himself or his side down when deputizing for Ian Botham against India and New Zealand. But tough, borderline decisions need to be made by all selectors and this committee, after making several mistakes in previous seasons, took two inspired decisions on this occasion.

There was a case for either Robert Russell, a quite brilliant wicket-keeper and an improving batsman, or Steve Rhodes, who had impressed everyone on the England 'B' tour of Sri Lanka, to go as reserve for Bruce French behind the stumps. But of the various other options the Selectors rejected the idea of taking Geoff Humpage or Alec Stewart, both outstanding batsmen but neither of Test class behind the stumps, and instead went for a tough, experienced cricketer who had always been respected in county cricket both as batsman and 'keeper: Jack Richards of Surrey. Few could have foreseen that he would immediately displace French; even fewer his dazzling hundred at Perth.

The other wise choice was that of Bill Athey, who started the tour with a Test batting average of 15 and only one 50 in eight matches. But Peter May had always liked Athey's attitude and technique, just as Gatting had always been impressed by Richards's potential. Their advocacy swung the argument in each case. On such hunches do the careers of professional cricketers ebb and flow.

For the England team itself, the time for a renewed 'flow' was near. But first there lay ahead of the 16 players, who had had only a brief rest at the end of the season, hard weeks of preparation before the opening roar of the cannon at Brisbane in November.

CHAPTER TWO

EARLY GLOOM

The England party, managed by Peter Lush, with Mickey Stewart in charge of their cricketing activities and Laurie Brown, the cheerful Scot from Musselburgh, looking after their aches and breaks (happily, in fact, there were to be few of the former and none of the latter), flew out of a slightly misty Heathrow airport on 9 October 1986.

In the contrasting humid warmth of Brisbane they spent five days of acclimatization, enjoying themselves in the evening at the convivial Crest Hotel and building a good early relationship with the Press, but by daylight sparing themselves little under Stewart's shrewd but firm guidance. It was quickly clear that in the former Surrey captain and England batsman, the TCCB had chosen a coach whose thoroughness and single-mindedness made him precisely the right man in the right place at the right time.

The tour began with a most encouraging display of the touring team's very considerable batting prowess in a three-day match against a Queensland Country XI at the rum-making town of Bundaberg, where the great Don Tallon learned his trade. In particular, Mike Gatting made a most positive announcement that he had come to do serious business in Australia, his dominating 171 being laced with several meaty sixes. He disappointed many by not enforcing a follow-on, enabling Bruce French to make an accomplished early 50, but England soon had the first win under their belt, in their second country match at Lawes, where Allan Lamb showed himself to be in imposing early-tour form.

The England touring team in Australia 1986–87, pictured with the Australian PM at the Manuka Oval, Canberra, two days before Christmas. Back row, left to right: S.P. Austin, M.J. Stewart, B.N. French, W.N. Slack, P.A.J. DeFreitas, B.C. Broad, G.C. Small, J.J. Whitaker, C.J. Richards, C.W.J. Athey, L. Brown. Front row, left to right: P.M. Lush, N.A. Foster, G.R. Dilley, D.I. Gower, Hon. R.J.L. Hawke, M.W. Gatting, I.T. Botham, A.J. Lamb, P.H. Edmonds. J.E. Emburey was taking a well earned rest during this match.

Facing the media. For Ian Botham the Press hounds gathered only for 'genuine' cricket stories. Early in the tour his decision to join Queensland and leave Somerset kept him in the news. Afterwards came the century at Brisbane, the back injury at Perth and success at Melbourne and in the one-dayers. But, happily, there was no muck to be raked.

Wilf Slack enjoyed his visit to Bundaberg but sadly failed in both innings against Queensland.

Opening matches against non-first-class opposition
18, 19, 20 October
BUNDABERG: England XI drew with Queensland Country XI. England XI 491/4 dec (B.C. Broad 97, W.N. Slack 70, C.W.J. Athey 73*, M.W. Gatting 171, I.T. Botham 52* and 129/3 (B.N. French 63*); Queensland Country XI 160 (L. Schulte 78*; P.A.J. DeFreitas 4 for 37)

22 October
LAWES: England XI beat South East Queensland Country XI by 58 runs. England XI 245/9 in 50 overs (A.J. Lamb 111*; S. Beattie 4 for 50); South East Queensland Country XI 187/6 in 50 overs

What followed, however, was a disappointing anti-climax. England suffered their first batting collapse of the tour in their opening first-class match. They immediately struggled against the left-arm-over bowlers, Frei and Tazelaar, and managed only 135 on a good batting wicket. Their bowlers then had to wait almost five hours for their first wicket as Kerr, a recent Test opener, and Courtice shared an opening stand of 154. Then Border made 47 in 80 minutes before declaring 176 ahead.

At 99 for five in their second innings, England looked in severe danger of an innings defeat, then Lamb and Botham launched a counter-attack with a stand of 122, Botham hitting 11 fours and four sixes in his 86, made in 66 balls, and Foster made a career-best as the last two wickets added 108. But Ritchie's 52 guaranteed Queensland victory and England's third defeat in the opening first class fixture in their last four Australian tours.

QUEENSLAND v ENGLAND XI

Played at Brisbane on 24, 25, 26, 27 October 1986
Toss: Queensland. Result: Queensland won by 5 wickets

ENGLAND XI

B.C. Broad	c Henschell b McDermott	7		b McDermott	18
W.N. Slack	c Anderson b Frei	1		c Henschell b Frei	0
D.I. Gower	c Ritchie b McDermott	20	(4)	c Kerr b Frei	17
A.J. Lamb	b Tazelaar	1	(5)	b McDermott	65
*M.W. Gatting	c Kerr b Frei	35	(6)	b Henschell	13
I.T. Botham	c Border b Tazelaar	9	(7)	c McDermott b Tazelaar	86
J.E. Emburey	lbw b Tazelaar	24	(8)	b McDermott	0
P.A.J. DeFreitas	c Kerr b Tazelaar	5	(9)	b Hill	22
†B.N. French	not out	11	(3)	c Kerr b McDermott	6
N.A. Foster	c Trimble b Henschell	2		not out	74
G.C. Small	c Tazelaar b Henschell	0		c Courtice b Hill	16
Extras	(b 1, lb 6, nb 13)	20		(lb 5, w 1, nb 16)	22
Total		135			339

QUEENSLAND

B.A. Courtice	c Lamb b Foster	70	(2)	b DeFreitas	23
R.B. Kerr	c Slack b Gatting	95	(1)	c Slack b Botham	8
G.S. Trimble	c French b DeFreitas	24		hit wkt b Botham	17
A.B. Henschell	c Gatting b Botham	3		not out	38
*A.R. Border	c Foster b Small	47	(7)	not out	10
†P.W. Anderson	c French b Small	20		c Small b Emburey	9
C.J. McDermott	c and b Small	18			
J.C. Hill	not out	13			
D. Tazelaar	not out	8			
G.M. Ritchie			(5)	run out	52
H. Frei					
Extras	(lb 9, nb 4)	13		(lb 6, nb 1)	7
Total	7 wickets declared	311		5 wickets	164

QUEENSLAND	O	M	R	W	O	M	R	W
McDermott	15	2	32	2	19	1	93	4
Frei	14	1	47	2	11	0	69	2
Tazelaar	14	4	34	4	14	1	60	1
Hill	6	5	9	0	10.2	1	31	2
Henschell	7.4	4	6	2	8	0	80	1
Courtice					1	0	1	0

ENGLAND XI	O	M	R	W	O	M	R	W
Botham	20	8	39	1	9	1	26	2
DeFreitas	26	5	61	1	13	3	40	1
Small	23	4	60	3	14.3	3	41	0
Foster	25	5	76	1	7	0	21	0
Emburey	20	4	63	0	7	2	30	1
Gatting	3	2	3	1				

FALL OF WICKETS

	E	Q	E	Q
Wkt	1st	1st	2nd	2nd
1st	14	154	4	18
2nd	37	188	27	36
3rd	40	204	47	65
4th	44	204	50	139
5th	57	251	99	150
6th	110	284	221	
7th	118	291	221	
8th	129		231	
9th	135		284	
10th	135		339	

Umpires: M.W. Johnson and C.D. Timmins.

If the main purpose of these early weeks of the tour was acclimatization, the tour planners certainly made the team work hard. The seventh of over 30 flights was, for those who took it, the most memorable. Two small aircraft, one carrying the team, the other a party of intrepid English and Australian journalists, took off from Adelaide for Wudinna and those who had to resort to use of the paper bags in front of their seats during a distinctly uneven journey, reflected, despite a warm local reception, that they 'wudinna' gone there unless they'd had to. England duly beat the Country XI but, at this stage of the tour at least – and despite the need to keep a few of the traditional country games in the modern tour itinerary – they should really have been taking on tougher, more demanding opposition and *less* demanding travel.

29 October
WUDINNA: England XI beat South Australia Country XI by nine wickets. South Australia Country XI 131/9 in 50 overs (J. Mitchell 68; N.A. Foster 3 for 22); England XI 135/1 in 33.4 overs (B.C. Broad 59, W.N. Slack 54*)

With only two more first-class matches before the first Test, the start against South Australia at the Adelaide Oval was vitally important, both for the morale of the team as a whole and for several individuals vying for Test places.

England had to work hard for their five-wicket victory but it was a reward for fine hundreds from Lamb and Whitaker and a marathon spell of bowling by Emburey. South Australia batted first and Wayne Phillips, keen to regain his Test place recently lost, made a vigorous 116, as he and Bishop added 144 for the third wicket. Then England had their best day of the tour so far, Lamb and Whitaker adding 172 in two and a half hours for the fourth wicket, having come together at 38 for three. The young Leicestershire batsman

joined a very select group who have scored a hundred in their first innings for England and in their first in Australia. Botham made 70 in 62 balls, again quickly finding his range. Sam Parkinson, another left-arm fast bowler, collected five wickets. Hookes hit 10 fours and two sixes in his second-innings hundred but Emburey's perseverance left England needing 168 to win. Broad, who became the first of the openers to make a sizeable score against first-class opposition on the tour, addèd 106 with Lamb, and Botham steered the side home.

Digging for gold? Phil Edmonds takes a break on the road to Kalgoorlie. The country games still have a place on a modern tour but too many were played in the early weeks of the tour when England needed less travel and more first-class matches.

After the long, unnecessary flight across the vast, arid continent, the England party spent a night in the gold-mining town of Kalgoorlie, last visited by Ted Dexter's team in 1962. It was Bill Athey who struck gold this time, playing a brilliant innings which was to become very significant when the tour selectors sat down to choose the team for the first Test in the wake of another very disappointing performance against Western Australia.

SOUTH AUSTRALIA v ENGLAND XI

Played at Adelaide on 31 October, 1, 2, 3 November 1986
Toss: South Australia. Result: England XI won by 5 wickets

SOUTH AUSTRALIA

Batsman	1st Innings		2nd Innings	
A.M.J. Hilditch	c Gatting b Small	11	b Botham	7
A.S. Watson	c Athey b Dilley	9	lbw b Dilley	1
W.B. Phillips	b Emburey	116	c and b Emburey	70
G.A. Bishop	b Edmonds	67	c Edmonds b Emburey	31
*D.W. Hookes	c Whitaker b Edmonds	0	c Richards b Emburey	104
P.R. Sleep	not out	66	b Emburey	27
†D.J. Kelly	c and b Emburey	4	c Gatting b Emburey	5
A.K. Zesers	b Emburey	1	c Edmonds b Emburey	1
T.B.A. Moy	c Richards b Botham	15	c Athey b Botham	2
S.D.H. Parkinson	not out	11	c Gatting b Dilley	6
P.W. Gladigau			not out	1
Extras	(lb 3, nb 2)	5	(b 4, lb 3, nb 7)	14
Total	8 wickets declared	305		269

ENGLAND XI

Batsman	1st Innings		2nd Innings	
B.C. Broad	lbw b Parkinson	0	c Phillips b Hookes	63
C.W.J. Athey	b Parkinson	18	c Kelly b Gladigau	0
*M.W. Gatting	c Kelly b Parkinson	8	c Kelly b Gladigau	4
A.J. Lamb	st Kelly b Sleep	105	c Sleep b Hookes	55
J.J. Whitaker	c Watson b Parkinson	108		
I.T. Botham	c Hookes b May	70	not out	19
†C.J. Richards	c Hookes b Sleep	24	(5) b Hookes	9
J.E. Emburey	st Kelly b May	4	(7) not out	10
P.H. Edmonds	c Hookes b Parkinson	27		
G.R. Dilley	c Kelly b Sleep	32		
G.C. Small	not out	0		
Extras	(b 5, lb 6)	11	(b 2, lb 2, w 4, nb 1)	9
Total		407	5 wickets	169

ENGLAND XI	O	M	R	W	O	M	R	W
Dilley	12	0	32	1	13	2	61	2
Botham	12	3	31	1	7.1	1	17	2
Emburey	33	8	76	3	38	11	102	6
Small	9	4	43	1				
Edmonds	29	5	97	2	36	10	82	0
Gatting	6	0	23	0	1	1	0	0

SOUTH AUSTRALIA	O	M	R	W	O	M	R	W
Gladigau	14	2	56	0	6	2	15	2
Parkinson	22.4	2	87	5	7	1	25	0
Zesers	23	6	77	0	4	0	15	0
May	23	0	111	2	1	0	9	0
Sleep	20	7	65	3	12	2	38	0
Hookes					15	5	58	3
Hilditch					1	0	1	0
Watson					0.2	0	4	0

FALL OF WICKETS

Wkt	SA 1st	E 1st	SA 2nd	E 2nd
1st	16	1	7	15
2nd	42	15	9	23
3rd	186	38	54	129
4th	186	210	199	130
5th	216	294	240	143
6th	224	325	256	
7th	234	347	257	
8th	283	347	257	
9th		407	265	
10th		407	269	

Umpires: A.R. Crafter and B.E. Martin.

A change from air-travel: Phil Edmonds, David Gower, Henry Blofeld, Scyld Berry and Peter West about to leave on the long rail journey from Adelaide (S. Australia) to Kalgoorlie in the west across the arid Nullarbor Plain.

5 November
KALGOORLIE: England XI beat Western Australia Country XI by 117 runs. England XI 293/5 in 50 overs (W.N. Slack 45, C.W.J. Athey 124, J.J. Whitaker 49); Western Australia Country XI 176/9 in 50 overs (C.W.J. Athey 3 for 40)

In the last match before the first Test in Brisbane Slack managed only 15 and nought. Gower completed a 'pair' and both Lamb and Gatting made ducks. Slack had so far managed 16 first-class runs (average 4.00), Gower 37 (9.25) and Gatting 79 (13.16) giving a distinctly insecure look to the batting line-up. In the second innings Gatting showed his lack of faith in poor Wilf Slack by sending Gladstone Small in to open the England first innings with only one over of the second day to go.

Small helped Broad to equal the highest opening stand – just 15! Their first confrontation with the six-foot-eight left-arm fast bowler Bruce Reid was disturbing and they also had difficulties with another left-armer, Chris Matthews. The Test opener Geoff Marsh looked ominously secure batting over five hours for his first-innings hundred, but Phillip DeFreitas bowled with impressive verve to take five wickets, one of them – that of the unfortunate Mike Veletta – with a ball of sudden, wicked, kicking pace. The West Indian blood in this personable young Englishman seems to give him that special ability to bowl the really fast ball and his vitality, athleticism and persistence in this match at the WACA undoubtedly made it certain that he would earn his first Test cap at the age of 20. Botham, putting aside thought of his Somerset future and also ignoring a damaged ankle, hammered 48 off 38 balls, then made a disciplined 40 not out to save the game after England had needed an unlikely 331 to win in four hours.

WESTERN AUSTRALIA v ENGLAND XI

Played at Perth on 7, 8, 9, 10 November 1986
Toss: England XI. Result: Match drawn

WESTERN AUSTRALIA

Batsman	1st innings		2nd innings	
G.R. Marsh	b Botham	124	lbw b Small	63
M.R.J. Veletta	c Gatting b Botham	10	c Broad b DeFreitas	2
T.M. Moody	c Richards b DeFreitas	19	st Richards b Edmonds	45
*G.M. Wood	c Botham b DeFreitas	9	c Gatting b Edmonds	53
W.S. Andrews	b Dilley	31	b Edmonds	9
K.H. Macleay	c Richards b DeFreitas	7	run out	10
†M.J. Cox	lbw b Dilley	1	run out	8
T.G. Breman	c Edmonds b DeFreitas	4	c sub (J.E. Emburey) b Gatting	0
C.D. Matthews	c Gower b Small	56	not out	3
B. Mulder	not out	1	not out	2
B.A. Reid	b Botham	0		
Extras	(lb 10, w 3)	13	(b 1, lb 4, nb 7)	12
Total		275	8 wickets declared	207

ENGLAND XI

Batsman	1st innings		2nd innings	
G.C. Small	b Matthews	3		
B.C. Broad	c Cox b Macleay	33	(1) c Macleay b Reid	25
W.N. Slack	b Reid	15	(2) c Moody b Macleay	0
D.I. Gower	b Reid	0	(3) c Wood b Macleay	0
A.J. Lamb	c Wood b Reid	0	(4) c and b Mulder	63
*M.W. Gatting	b Matthews	19	(5) c Wood b Reid	0
†C.J. Richards	c Cox b Reid	3	(6) c Cox b Mulder	17
I.T. Botham	c Reid b Breman	48	(7) not out	40
P.A.J. DeFreitas	c Cox b Matthews	20	(8) not out	3
P.H. Edmonds	b Matthews	1		
G.R. Dilley	not out	1		
Extras	(b 1, lb 1, nb 7)	9	(lb 1, w 2, nb 2)	5
Total		152	6 wickets	153

ENGLAND XI	O	M	R	W	O	M	R	W
Dilley	16	4	43	2	14	0	38	0
DeFreitas	22	5	82	4	14	2	51	1
Small	18	4	67	1	15	3	44	1
Botham	14.4	1	42	3	8	2	31	0
Edmonds	9	1	31	0	13	1	37	3
Gatting					1	0	1	1

WESTERN AUSTRALIA	O	M	R	W	O	M	R	W
Reid	11	3	40	4	6	3	15	2
Macleay	16	9	34	1	7	3	26	2
Matthews	14.5	3	30	4	11	2	23	0
Breman	7	1	40	1	13	3	30	0
Mulder	2	1	6	0	16	5	46	2
Moody					3	2	2	0
Veletta					1	0	10	0

FALL OF WICKETS

Wkt	WA 1st	E 1st	WA 2nd	E 2nd
1st	30	15	18	1
2nd	66	56	90	5
3rd	102	56	164	53
4th	163	56	178	54
5th	176	57	186	95
6th	185	69	196	134
7th	190	128	202	
8th	274	134	203	
9th	275	151		
10th	275	152		

Umpires: C. Cannon and P.J. McConnell.

Not again! David Gower is a picture of dejection as he walks out after one of his deceptive early-tour failures.

England's performances leading up to the first Test had been extremely disappointing and, as a result, they went into it in a poor mental state in some cases – notably the apparently drifting and world-weary David Gower – and with few of the pundits giving them much chance. I was less pessimistic, feeling that the Test-match atmosphere would concentrate the minds of England's hitherto struggling but potentially powerful batting combination, especially as the Australian selectors had chosen a very inexperienced and largely unproven group of bowlers in Mervyn Hughes, Bruce Reid, Chris Matthews and Greg Matthews, with Steven Waugh in support.

It is not unusual, in any case, for England sides in Australia to start badly and then end the tour triumphant. Ray Illingworth's side in 1970–71 is a case in point and Illingworth himself has said in *Test Match Special* that he reckoned it was nearly Christmas by the time his side was firing on all cylinders.

The unfortunate thing this time was that by Christmas the Test series would virtually be decided, so the failure to move out of first gear, especially but not exclusively in the batting department in the major games, *was* worrying. It had been a collective failure, although some had done better than others, notably the two young bloods, Phillip DeFreitas and James Whitaker, whose century at Adelaide opened up for him visions of glory which, alas, were not to be realized on a tour which left him increasingly frustrated and inactive. The experience will only have hardened his resolve when the chance comes again.

Two questions needed answering at the end of the first phase of the tour: first, why had England failed several times against left-arm over-the-wicket fast bowlers; and secondly, why had they travelled so far and so often and yet played so little first-class cricket?

To take the programme first. The team left England on 9 October and no fewer than five weeks later had played only 12 days of first-class cricket. Having appreciated the need for a month's acclimatization, the tour planners fitted in at least one four-day match too few. The likes of Doug Insole and Donald Carr must have known how inadequate this was. Why did they agree to the programme and why were the Tests at Perth and Brisbane not switched to save 4,000 unnecessary miles and a two-hour jet lag each way?

Country games still have a part to play on tours of Australia. They are festive occasions for the local communities, valuable flag-flying exercises for the game, and educational for the visiting players who might get the impression otherwise that Australia is a country of cities, airports and cricket grounds. The mining town of Kalgoorlie was especially interesting and its gold mines are booming these days as they have not boomed for many a year. The air journey to the outpost of Wudinna was memorable for different reasons. But the cricket played there was meaningless in terms of preparation for a Test match.

Even the opening three-day match at Bundaberg was probably letting the players in a little too gently. Mike Gatting would have gladly swapped his barnstorming 171 for even a couple of fifties during the first-innings collapses at Brisbane, Adelaide and Perth. England recovered handsomely in the middle game, against South Australia, thanks to brilliant batting by Whitaker and Allan Lamb, but the first-innings performances at the Gabba and the WACA might have been calculated to boost Australian morale. Some players failed through a careless lack of application, others through poor technique. And the common denominator, as it was when they lost three wickets for 38 in Adelaide, was a failure to deal with the left-arm-over swing bowling.

There are not many bowlers of this type in county cricket: John Lever and Roger Finney come to mind. Both can bowl the inswinger but neither is as swift or as hostile as the six-foot-eight Reid (a bag of sticks to look at, but a fine bowler with an ideal body action) or the tall and muscular Matthews. There are six such bowlers playing regular Sheffield Shield cricket and a long tradition of them in Australia. It is a tradition which looked like continuing with both Reid and Matthews selected for the first Test match at the Wooloongabba cricket ground in Brisbane.

Sandbags for defence? Peter Lush, the England manager, looks anxious on the eve of the first Test at Brisbane. Soon, most of his worries were behind him.

The preliminaries were over and the day for which the England team had prepared so hard was about to dawn.

CHAPTER THREE

THE GABBA:
PROPHETS CONFOUNDED!

On the eve of the first Test in Brisbane, the fledgling correspondent of the newly created London newspaper, *The Independent,* made an instant name for himself with a glib but memorable phrase which was gleefully repeated back in the Australian papers and was destined to be repeated time and time again during the remainder of the tour. 'England,' wrote Martin Johnson, 'have just one problem: they can't bat, they can't bowl and they can't field.'

BBC correspondent to skipper: 'Can England *really* win after such a start, Mike?' Gatting may not have been the most eloquent of interviewees but he was always honest and positive with the media and soon won their respect.

Well, the 1986–87 England touring team gave both themselves and their critics (who are benevolent souls, really) a pleasant surprise by batting, bowling *and* fielding much better than Australia to win the Brisbane Test by seven comfortable wickets.

When last they had won at the Gabba, by an exactly similar margin, they had gone on to win the Ashes under Mike Brearley. Ian Botham, David Gower and Phil Edmonds were three survivors of that victory in 1978 – John Emburey was on the tour but Geoff Miller was preferred at Brisbane – and in the wars ahead they were to help history to repeat itself.

To have won after so modest a start to the tour and, even more to the point, after losing a toss which both sides had dreaded, was an extraordinary achievement worthy of the highest praise. Not since 1974 had a side batting first in a Brisbane Test match scored more than 300 and, even then, I recall, it was only a last-wicket stand which enabled Australia to get past 300 before Lillee and Thomson got going with the ball. This time a pitch which was moist at the start but not so fast and not so dangerous as expected; determined and often brilliant England batting; and wayward bowling by the most inexperienced Australian attack since the one commanded by Yallop in 1978, conspired to build England a match-winning first innings total of 456.

Marvellously accurate spin bowling by Emburey, well supported by Phil Edmonds and disciplined fast bowling by Graham Dilley, Botham and Phil

DeFreitas, made sure that the golden opportunity was not wasted. Soon after lunch on the fifth day, with even the weather supporting England, a crowd of little more than a thousand witnessed England's first win in 12 Tests in 1986, their first in six under the captaincy of Gatting and yet their third in a row against Australia.

The first two days of the match could hardly have gone better for England after their indifferent start to the tour and the unfortunate loss of the toss. England had taken the brave decision to include both their spin bowlers, gambling to some extent on batting first, although there was enough moisture in the pitch for the spinners to have got some help early in the game as well as when the pitch became worn. In the event, Border won the toss for the eighth successive time and took what turned out to be a mistaken decision, though Gatting would surely have made the same error: he chose to bowl first. That the pitch was helpful to the seam bowlers was not in doubt, but Broad had needed to play at very little when in the ninth over he nibbled at Reid and nicked to the wicket-keeper.

After much discussion, and on the firmly expressed advice of Allan Lamb, England reverted at the last minute, after a debate in the lavatory, to the batting order which had been so successful in India, Gatting coming in at number three instead of Gower, whose mood was unhappy and form uncertain and whose place, indeed, was in some danger from James Whitaker. Gatting's start was by no means assured but by lunchtime he was well settled, having cover-driven, square-cut and hooked four fours in his 31 out of England's 65 for one. Two more thumping hooks off Chris Matthews, tending to pitch too short on his first day in Test cricket, set the pattern for the afternoon.

Bill Athey, neat and careful in defence, and gradually trusting himself to pull or hook the short deliveries and to push firmly through the half-volleys, was content to stay in his captain's bulky shadow, putting together an innings which did much both for his own confidence and for that of team-mates watching with increasing pleasure as the threat of collapse turned into the expectation of a big total. Gatting's 50 included nine fours and he was just taking complete control, having driven Hughes through extra-cover and hooked him boldly back over his head in successive balls, when he was unlucky to be bowled off his pads.

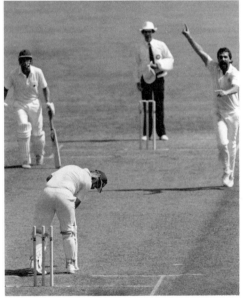

Captain's innings aborted: Mervyn Hughes bowls Mike Gatting off his pads after his pugnacious opening salvo at the Gabba.

There were no worries about Lamb's form, only a fear that he might get himself out through over-confidence. But his judgement was as good as his timing and he and Athey took England to 198 for two before a heavy shower ended play for the day (after one previous brief interruption) 22 overs early.

Hughes, a strong, genuinely fast, whole-hearted, unsubtle bowler, and Matthews, tall, strapping and blessed with the left-arm-over bowler's most valuable gift, an inswinger, hit back with a wicket apiece in the first four overs of the second day. Lamb was leg before, half-forward, to the day's first ball, which had the virtue of being straight but it took a particularly good ball, and an especially good catch, to dismiss Athey off the inside edge.

England now had the great good luck to have Gower dropped at third slip off Hughes before he had scored. His start was altogether sketchy and perilous, in contrast to Botham who entered the arena bare-headed, confident and almost patronizing to all the young Australians around him. He was not beaten, so far as one could detect, all day, except when occasionally he slogged and missed. He played himself in with patience, and some 20 minutes before lunch suddenly unleashed a formidable volley of strokes, hitting three effortless fours in one over from Reid, one a straight drive and two chipped to mid-wicket off his toes.

The end of a dogged and important innings. Bill Athey caught by Tim Zoehrer off Chris Matthews for 76 early on the second day at Brisbane.

One that got away. The Australian slip catching was fallible throughout the series and the dropping of Gower when nought in the first Test was possibly crucial to its outcome. Left to right: Boon, Border and Zoehrer.

The bombardment by Ian Botham broke Australia's brief fight-back on the second morning; here he puts everything into a hook during this thunderous innings of 138. Note, no helmet.

Phillip DeFreitas during his ideal attacking innings at Brisbane. Thereafter he seldom showed what he was capable of with the bat.

The roles were reversed for a short while after lunch with Gower starting to play altogether more solidly, his off-side strokes going to mid-off rather than gully and runs being picked up fluently off his legs, while Botham struggled awhile to retrieve his timing. But Gower, who had already played a couple of his famous swivel-footed pulls through mid-wicket, was well caught attempting another, hit right out of the middle of the bat. This, his favourite stroke, is both his most productive and his most self-destructive. He never has been, and never will be, able to resist it.

Botham was on 62 when this happened and Border now settled for a policy of giving him singles to a deep-set field, meanwhile attacking his partners. It seldom pays to offer the initiative to any batsman and Botham certainly wasn't complaining. Whilst Emburey was at the wicket he scored a good many twos by dabbing the ball well short of the eight boundary fielders and when DeFreitas joined him runs soon began to flow again from both ends.

Botham reached his hundred shortly before tea with a cut and a straight drive for twos off the first two balls of an over from Hughes and he celebrated by hooking the next one for six, then hooking and on-driving three more crashing fours in the next three balls – 22 from one over and all this by a local Brisbane boy! It was a shame indeed that fewer than 8,000 people were there to see him.

At Cambridge University a group of undergraduates took pity on Hughes, and instantly formed the 'Mervyn' Club. It became quite fashionable as the series progressed. Whether Hughes was fully aware of his fame in a distant seat of learning, I am not sure.

Botham finally top-edged a hook but not before he had helped DeFreitas to launch his Test batting career with a vigorous, confident innings which saw England past 450. In just over an hour's batting before the close of the second day, Australia replied with 33 for the loss of Boon, who obligingly pulled DeFreitas to mid-wicket.

England bowled with admirable accuracy and persistence throughout a clear, sunny Sunday, for much of which Gatting bowled his three fast bowlers with the wind blowing over their right shoulders from the Stanley Street End whilst first Emburey – at length – and then Edmonds – more briefly – wheeled away accurately from the other. Dilley, consistently the most dangerous, took five for 68, his first five-wicket haul for England in this his 22nd Test, seven years after his first appearance at Perth on the 1979–80 tour.

Dilley's first wicket of the day came when Zoehrer, after an enterprising and capable night-watchman's innings, went back and was lbw for 38. Jones was also lbw, to DeFreitas, who soon after lunch produced an out-swinger to remove the adhesive Marsh for 56 made in just under four and half hours.

Dean Jones took time to fathom the subtle variations of John Emburey. A close call in the second innings at Brisbane was followed by an unavailing charge, allowing Jack Richards to make his first Test stumping.

Potential at last fulfilled: Graham Dilley during his first five-wicket hand in Tests. A fine study in poise and concentration.

Ritchie was the first positively to attack the bowling, moving down the pitch to drive Emburey over mid-wicket for six, but when Border tried something similar off Edmonds he sliced a catch to cover. England took the new ball at the first opportunity two overs after tea, and Dilley had Ritchie caught in the gully for 41 and Waugh caught behind for nought, both from balls which lifted and swung away. Thereafter it was Greg Matthews, relishing every moment of the fight against England, who edged Australia towards the follow-on figure. He made an unbeaten 56, but a tiring Botham and Dilley were too good for the tail and Australia were all-out nine runs short of saving the follow-on.

England's toughest day was the fourth. It was sultry, hot and humid and they were lucky that a storm confidently predicted by local weather forecasters somehow forbore to break. Two of the five wickets to fall during a long day in which England bowled 102 overs, 12 more than the necessary quota (and they would have been fined had they not bowled 90), went down in the last hour when the expected rain might so easily have fallen.

Australia's hero on their one really hopeful day of the match was the 27-year-old farmer from the tiny township of Wandering, where there is not much more than a pub, a store and a few families, including a grain and sheep farmer named Ted Marsh and his son Geoff. It has taken Marsh longer than it takes most outstanding young Australians to get an extended chance in Test cricket – after all, he made a hundred for their schoolboy side as long ago as 1977, at Lord's of all places – but his six-hour century was his third in only 10 Tests and his second in successive ones. He made remarkably few errors all day on a pitch which remained very friendly to the batsmen. His technique, developed by practice against a bowling machine in that distant outpost, is simple and orthodox. He gets behind the ball, plays it late and has his head firmly over the top of the leather at the moment of impact. He also leaves a lot of what he does not need to play.

Got you! Ian Botham appeals successfully for lbw against the luckless David Boon in the second innings.

'Swampy' Marsh played throughout the series with admirable resolution and excellent technique. There was much relief when he played-on off Philip DeFreitas for 110 early on the final morning at the Gabba.

England bowled a good, consistent line and length all day, but were looking a little worried and naturally weary when tea arrived with the obdurate Marsh still in untroubled possession of the crease, in company with Ritchie, who remains a gifted batsman more liable than most to self-destruct. Not that he did so on this occasion, but DeFreitas's wicket, from his first delivery with the new ball, was the most important of the five he took on his happy Test début.

Five wickets in the day was probably the minimum required by England and the last one came when Greg Matthews, who plays mainly square of the wicket on either side, turned his wrists a fraction early as he tried to clip Dilley to leg and gave a caught and bowled off the leading edge. Work remained to be done, but England could sleep more easily now, even though Waugh remained to disturb

their peace – so to speak.

As so often happens after a long resistance by a side fighting to save a match, the wall, once breached, collapsed quite suddenly. For the first half an hour of the fifth day, a beautifully fresh, breezy and sunny one after the heavy humidity of Tuesday, Marsh and, in particular, Waugh batted with some confidence. Fifteen came off the first two overs from DeFreitas and Dilley, Waugh playing two crisp square-cuts, and there was much relief for England when Marsh, push-driving towards extra-cover, got an inside edge into his stumps. He had batted over six and a half hours for his 110 and 10 minutes under 20 hours in his four innings against England so far on the tour.

Two more wickets fell in the next seven balls as Emburey beat Waugh in flight and bowled him for 28, and had Chris Matthews leg-before, pushing forward.

Victory approaches: Steve Waugh bowled by Emburey for 28. The selectors wisely stuck by the talented Waugh despite early calls for his execution in the Australian Press.

Australia were now clearly doomed with only the capable Zoehrer and two genuine tail-enders to come. DeFreitas and Emburey picked up a wicket each, Emburey finishing with five for 80 to confirm his reputation as one of England's finest off-spin bowlers, especially overseas. His first wicket of the morning was his hundredth in Test matches, taken at a striking rate superior not just to Edmonds, but also, amongst off-spinners of recent times, to David Allen, Ray Illingworth and Fred Titmus who took a wicket respectively every 92, 97 and 98 balls against Emburey's 86.

On the whole, though it is not true of the current Australians, tail-enders take their batting more seriously than they once did and Emburey, unlike Underwood, whose 297 Test wickets came at a rate of one every 73 balls, has bowled only on covered pitches. He was the only England bowler – the only player indeed – who had returned from the Caribbean earlier in the year with his reputation enhanced. He took 14 wickets at 32 there in the Tests and but for Viv Richards he would have had much better figures still. Richards never let him settle. In this match at Brisbane, the reverse was the case. Emburey never let the Australian batsmen dictate the terms.

England lost three wickets in getting the 75 they needed to win, Hughes picking up the first two, that of Athey with the help of a brilliant slip catch by Waugh, who had earlier missed Broad off the same bowler. Broad made no further errors and hit the winning runs in company with a Gower batting at his brilliant best; one remarkable shot past mid-on off Greg Matthews – after he had been beaten in the air – bore testimony to his rediscovered genius. England, like Gower, seemed born again!

AUSTRALIA v ENGLAND (First Test)

Played at Brisbane on 14, 15, 16, 18, 19 November 1986
Toss: Australia. Result: England won by seven wickets. Man of the match: I. T. Botham

ENGLAND

B.C. Broad	c Zoehrer b Reid	8	not out		35
C.W.J. Athey	c Zoehrer b C.D. Matthews	76	c Waugh b Hughes		1
*M.W. Gatting	b Hughes	61	c G.R.J. Mathews b Hughes		12
A.J. Lamb	lbw b Hughes	40	lbw b Reid		9
D.I. Gower	c Ritchie b C.D. Matthews	51	not out		15
I. T. Botham	c Hughes b Waugh	138			
†C.J. Richards	b C.D. Matthews	0			
J.E. Emburey	c Waugh b Hughes	8			
P.A.J. DeFreitas	c C.D. Matthews b Waugh	40			
P.H. Edmonds	not out	9			
G.R. Dilley	c Boon b Waugh	0			
Extras	(b 3, lb 19, nb 3)	25	(b 2, nb 3)		5
Total		456	3 wickets		77

AUSTRALIA

G.R. Marsh	c Richards b Dilley	56	(2) b DeFreitas		110
D.C. Boon	c Broad b DeFreitas	10	(1) lbw b Botham		14
†T.J. Zoehrer	lbw b Dilley	38	(8) not out		16
D.M. Jones	lbw b DeFreitas	8	(3) st Richards b Emburey		18
*A.R. Border	c DeFreitas b Edmonds	7	(4) c Lamb b Emburey		23
G.M. Ritchie	c Edmonds b Dilley	41	(5) lbw b DeFreitas		45
G.R.J. Matthews	not out	56	(6) c and b Dilley		13
S.R. Waugh	c Richards b Dilley	0	(7) b Emburey		28
C.D. Matthews	c Gatting b Botham	11	lbw b Emburey		0
M.G. Hughes	b Botham	0	b DeFreitas		0
B.A. Reid	c Richards b Dilley	3	c Broad b Emburey		2
Extras	(b 2, lb 8, w 2, nb 6)	18	(b 5, lb 6, nb 2)		13
Total		248			282

AUSTRALIA	O	M	R	W	O	M	R	W		FALL OF WICKETS			
Reid	31	4	86	1	6	1	20	1		E	A	A	E
Hughes	36	7	134	3	5.3	0	28	2	*Wkt*	*1st*	*1st*	*2nd*	*2nd*
C.D. Matthews	35	10	95	3	4	0	11	0	1st	15	27	24	6
Waugh	21	3	76	3					2nd	116	97	44	25
G.R.J. Matthews	11	2	43	0	7	1	16	0	3rd	198	114	92	40
									4th	198	126	205	
ENGLAND	O	M	R	W	O	M	R	W	5th	316	159	224	
DeFreitas	16	5	32	2	17	2	62	3	6th	324	198	262	
Dilley	25.4	7	68	5	19	6	47	1	7th	351	204	266	
Emburey	34	11	66	0	42.5	14	80	5	8th	443	239	266	
Edmonds	12	6	12	1	24	8	46	0	9th	451	239	275	
Botham	16	1	58	2	12	0	34	1	10th	456	248	282	
Gatting	1	0	2	0	2	0	2	0					

Umpires: A.R. Crafter and M.W. Johnson.

The strife is o'er, the battle's won. Edmonds, Dilley, Broad, Botham, Slack, Gatting, Emburey, Athey, Whitaker, Richards, Brown (physio) and DeFreitas enjoy the traditional celebration.

CHAPTER FOUR

PERTH: OPPORTUNITY MISSED

A cartoon on the front page of the Murdoch national paper, *The Australian,* summed up the generally rather cynical Press reaction to Australia's seven-wicket defeat in the first Test at Brisbane. It depicted Allan Border barking at a laconic-looking journalist: 'I'm sick of you knockers in the media – haven't I won eight tosses in a row?' Indeed he had, which only made his setbacks seem worse.

The Press were calling Border 'grumpy' and this is exactly what he unfortunately was, for a few days at least, in reaction not so much to his team's poor performance and England's excellent one as to the widespread criticisms of his captaincy.

Grumpy? Allan Border felt the full weight of his countrymen's disapproval after the Brisbane defeat and took some unfair flak.

It was unfair to blame the captain for Australia's poor recent record when his own batting had so often saved them from total collapse in the previous two years. He is not, it is true, a very imaginative captain, but if his bowlers would not bowl consistently straight to a good length, as England's, with Emburey and Dilley to the fore, certainly did at Brisbane, it was not the captain's fault. Border's problem was, probably, that he was tired and that tired people get angry. He should not have been asked to lead an eight-week tour to India immediately before a long, arduous season at home. And he probably should not have played a season for Essex before that.

England travelled to the coastal industrial town of Newcastle for their four-day match against New South Wales, happy to let Australia worry about their problems and determined to build on their good start to the Test series. Any danger of complacency ought to have been banished by a reminder that no opening partnership in eight first-class innings on tour had so far exceeded 15. Four of the players who missed the match at the Gabba, Foster, French, Slack and Small, all played against a New South Wales team which included two bowlers anxious to catch the eyes of the Australian selectors, Geoff Lawson and Mike Whitney.

In the event it was Whitney and David Gilbert, another discarded Test bowler, who were chiefly responsible for inflicting on England a positively embarrassing defeat, their first against New South Wales since the 1962–63 tour.

England were put into bat on the coldest day of the whole tour. They had arrived on a small 'plane the day before, when the coastline around Newcastle had looked exactly like Cornwall in February. Perhaps the shock of such conditions after the humid heat of Brisbane partly excused England's inadequate first-innings score of 197, although damp patches on the pitch were a more genuine reason. The best batsmen, bar none, were the unjustly treated Bruce French, who played with pluck, skill and resource for 38 not out, and Neil Foster, who further added to his batting laurels until top-edging a hook at Lawson.

New South Wales were already in trouble at 15 for two by the end of the first day and, with French taking four catches and also producing a neat stumping, they were bowled out for 181 despite a cleanly struck 47 by Waugh and a doughty innings by the universally popular and respected Bob Holland, who relished his duties as night-watchman and batted through the morning for 34 not out.

This was the prelude to an extraordinary afternoon's cricket in which 14 wickets fell in two sessions and England virtually threw the game away. Gilbert and Whitney bowled fast and straight on a two-paced but far from unplayable pitch. The heroes of Brisbane went a little shamefacedly to their Saturday night's entertainment after finishing the day at 66 for nine.

Dirk Wellham duly hit the winning run just after half-past two on Sunday afternoon after both sides had appeared deliberately to contrive to deprive a crowd of 4,000 of an exhibition limited-overs match which they had been promised should the main match have finished sooner. It is an unfortunate characteristic of professional cricketers that they seek to play as little cricket as possible!

In fact, in this particular game, England's team had been rather *un*professional in their approach. But we all knew that this match and its result would soon be forgotten as long as England went on dominating the Test matches.

Having reacted nobly to losing the toss at Brisbane, England's unchanged Test team, unconcerned by the setback against New South Wales, made absolutely the most of winning the second toss of the series, in Perth. The combination of a superb pitch for batting and some wayward Australian bowling, especially but not exclusively in the crucial early stages, enabled Chris Broad and Bill Athey to put on 223 for the first wicket, the fourth largest opening stand by England against Australia.

From this cast-iron base, due especially to Broad's commanding innings, which at the very least established him for

Victor Ludorum: Chris Broad acknowledges the applause for his effortlessly gathered first Test hundred at Perth.

NEW SOUTH WALES v ENGLAND XI

Played at Newcastle on 21, 22, 23 November 1986
Toss: New South Wales. Result: New South Wales won by eight wickets

ENGLAND XI

Batsman	First Innings	Runs	Second Innings	Runs
B.C. Broad	lbw b Whitney	31	lbw b Gilbert	0
C.W.J. Athey	lbw b Lawson	3	lbw b Whitney	0
W.N. Slack	b Whitney	16	b Gilbert	18
D.I. Gower	c Wellham b Matthews	16	(5) c Holland b Whitney	0
J.J. Whitaker	c and b Matthews	4	(4) c Waugh b Whitney	6
*J.E. Emburey	c Waugh b Holland	10	(8) c Dyer b Whitney	6
I.T. Botham	c Taylor b Holland	14	(6) b Gilbert	6
P.H. Edmonds	b Matthews	6	(9) not out	17
†B.N. French	not out	38	(7) lbw b Whitney	0
N.A. Foster	c and b Lawson	25	b Holland	0
G.C. Small	b Holland	26	lbw b Gilbert	14
Extras	(b 3, lb 2, nb 3)	8	(lb 10, nb 5)	15
Total		**197**		**82**

NEW SOUTH WALES

Batsman	First Innings	Runs	Second Innings	Runs
S.M. Small	c Edmonds b Emburey	8	c Edmonds b Foster	9
M.A. Taylor	st French b Emburey	4	c Slack b Edmonds	31
R.G. Holland	c French b Edmonds	36		
*D.M. Wellham	lbw b Foster	18	(3) not out	29
M.D.O'Neill	b Foster	0	(4) not out	13
G.R.J. Matthews	b Emburey	25		
S.R. Waugh	c French b Small	47		
†G.C. Dyer	b Edmonds	4		
G.F. Lawson	c French b Small	26		
D.R. Gilbert	not out	10		
M.R. Whitney	c French b Foster	1		
Extras	(lb 1, nb 1)	2	(b 12, lb 3, nb 2)	17
Total		**181**	**2 wickets**	**99**

NEW SOUTH WALES	O	M	R	W	O	M	R	W
Lawson	16	3	42	2	4	3	2	0
Gilbert	5	1	16	0	14.4	3	26	4
Holland	27.3	11	58	3	2	1	5	1
Whitney	13	4	31	2	17	4	39	5
Matthews	19	6	33	3				
Waugh	5	0	12	0				

ENGLAND XI	O	M	R	W	O	M	R	W
Small	17	7	23	2	1	0	5	0
Foster	15.4	6	30	3	13.1	7	24	1
Emburey	29	9	65	3	15	7	16	0
Edmonds	31	13	55	2	16	4	32	1
Botham	2	0	7	0	3	1	7	0

FALL OF WICKETS

Wkt	E 1st	NSW 1st	E 2nd	NSW 2nd
1st	16	12	0	23
2nd	51	15	0	57
3rd	61	43	22	
4th	74	43	22	
5th	75	86	24	
6th	97	110	25	
7th	106	118	37	
8th	106	165	53	
9th	142	170	57	
10th	197	181	82	

Umpires: R.A. French and A.G. Marshall.

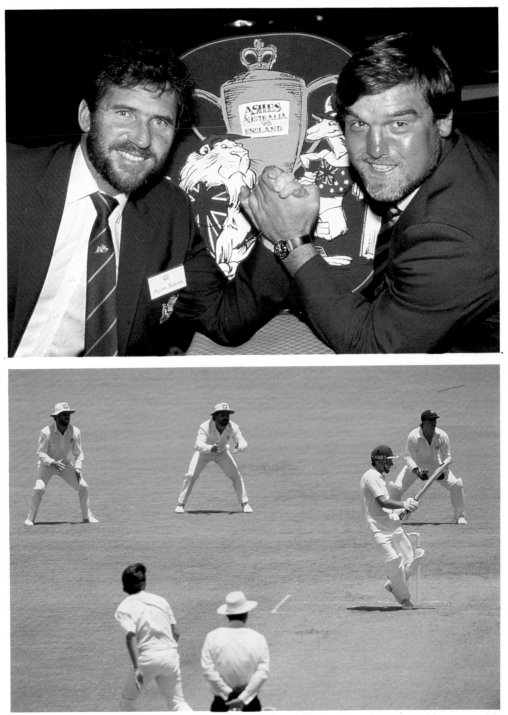

Top: Friendly trial of strength. The captains at a Benson and Hedges reception before the first Test.

Above: Bill Athey's dogged innings at Brisbane was crucial. Here he hooks Waugh to the boundary watched by first slip Boon, second slip Border, wicket-keeper Zoehrer and umpire Mal Johnson.

Over the bowler's head. Ian Botham unleashes one of his
authentic straight drives off Chris Matthews during his
swashbuckling 138 at the Gabba.

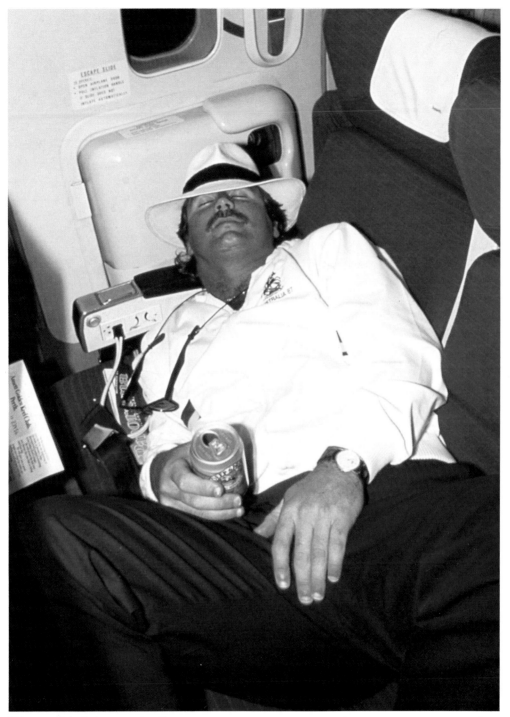

Thirty-two flights had an enervating effect on everyone.
Allan Lamb looks less alert than usual on the long haul west
from Brisbane to Perth after the first Test. (But he is still
keeping a careful guard on his priorities!)

The mass appeal of cricket? Left to right, Lamb, Gatting,
Botham, Emburey. A nice one, too, for the sponsors' album.

Lean and hungry. The stream-lined Bruce Reid in his
delivery stride. He was consistently the steadiest and most
dangerous of the Australian fast bowlers.

A sight which reduced Australians to chronic ambivalence.
David Gower has been at once a thorn in their flesh and a
joy to behold. This stroke brought him a characteristic
boundary during his hundred at Perth.

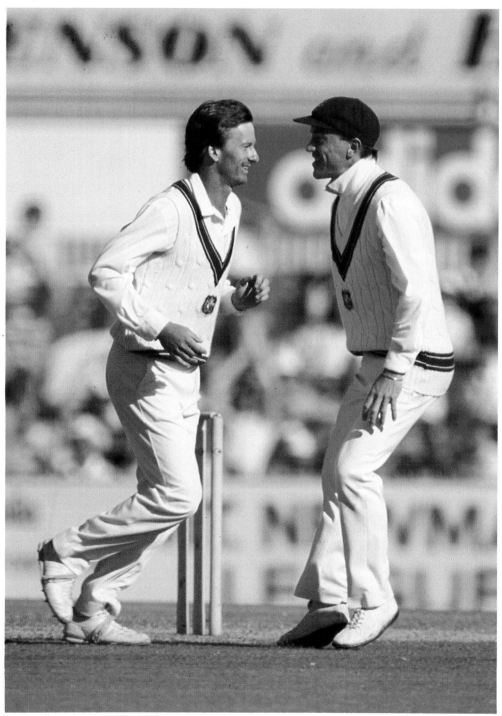

Genuine all-rounders? Steve Waugh (left) proved himself a batsman of genuine class and bowled a particularly valuable spell at Perth. But the ebullient Greg Matthews (right) had a disappointing series after being voted Player of the Year in Australia in 1985-86.

the rest of the tour, but which also opened up far-reaching possibilities for the rest of his career, not excluding the England captaincy should circumstances in due course change, England were able to declare just short of 600, 40 minutes from the end of the second day, despite ducks from Botham and Lamb, hitherto the highest scorers on the tour! David Gower, pulling, cutting and cover-driving his way back to mental happiness – and to his sixth Test hundred against Australia – found an unexpectedly confident ally in Jack Richards who, in only his second Test innings for his country, rubbed stinging salt into Australian wounds with an innings of belligerence, bottle and brilliance.

David Gower and Jack Richards capitalized gloriously on the early profits made by Broad and Athey. Gower, as usual, was majestic on the offside; Richards was ruggedly effective to the on.

For the last three days the match therefore hung on the question of whether or not England could bowl Border's team out twice on a pitch which reflected great credit on one of the world's most dedicated groundsmen, John Maley.

In the end the groundsman won, but it was touch and go whether Australia would avoid the follow-on and even on the last day there were moments when England had chances of forcing a victory. But although the pitch took on the appearance, close to, of a huge jigsaw puzzle with the biggest cracks I have seen since Sabina Park in 1973–74 (another drawn game), it remained rock hard and, by care and determination, Australia, aided by faulty England tactics, managed to draw and so to keep the series very much alive.

Whether, as he claimed, Mr Maley would really have been unable to prepare so good a wicket if he had been obliged to produce one also for a four-day game against the State in the week before the Test – as Australian groundsmen have traditionally done – is an interesting question. If he honestly could not have done, despite the considerable width of his square and the ideal climatic conditions in which he has to work, it means that all touring teams in future will be obliged to cross the huge island continent twice more than is necessary. England's players will no doubt feel that it was worth the extra hours' flying, and accompanying jet lag, though they might not have felt the same way if they had lost the toss!

As it happened it was raining in Brisbane for much of the time that the second Test was played, thus ruining the Sheffield Shield game between Queensland and West Australia, so, had the two venues been switched, the Gabba Test might have been a frustrating waste of time.

Maley's stated intention before the match, in a country where groundsmen in recent years have too often left the pitch too damp to start with, was to have a good batting wicket for the first day. It was obvious even three days before the game began that he had succeeded handsomely for its surface of even grass looked light brown and, under slow, heavy rolling, it was already becoming flat and true. Imagine English joy, therefore, when Gatting called correctly and Broad, tall, still and impeccably straight-batted, and Athey, like the terrier out walking with the great dane, moved the score past 50 in the first 15 overs.

The bowling of both Lawson and Matthews was woeful: ball after ball sprayed so wide of the stumps that a stroke did not even have to be contemplated. But they might have put the nervous start behind them if Athey, driving at a wide ball from Matthews when only three not out, had not been dropped by Border at third slip.

Broad reached his third 50 in his seventh match for England with a force off the back foot past the bowler, Chris Matthews, and at the other end immediately gave his one half-chance of the day when Lawson could not quite stretch far enough to take a low return catch. In the same over Broad drove him through mid-on and mid-wicket for boundaries to reassert his stately command.

Athey was neat, determined, but more vulnerable. He escaped another quite tricky chance to square-leg (Jones) off Reid, much the tidiest and most menacing of the bowlers, when he was 46, then straight drove him to reach his second 50 of the series. This seemed to relax him. He showed a special liking for the off-spin of the senior Matthews and by tea was starting to catch his partner. England were 187 for no wicket, Broad 98, Athey 72.

Broad's simple, straight-bat technique – no hooking and seldom even a

The *other* Matthews! More may yet be heard of the powerfully built Chris Matthews from W. Australia. His selection came too soon, perhaps, but his athleticism was plain to see.

square-cut – and genuine hunger for runs made it certain that, though he would never make an easier Test hundred, he would soon be adding to the one he now reached with a sweetly timed stroke off Greg Matthews, his 17th four.

Athey, on the other hand, may never have a better chance to record a Test century in the most satisfying of all circumstances for any English player: against Australia, in Australia. He escaped a sliced cut to Boon at slip off Greg Matthews when 91 but was then deceived by a superb, slightly slower in-swinging yorker from Reid.

Lamb came in ahead of Gatting – these two and Gower had been rotating in the dressing-room rather than having one man padded up at the ready all day – and, going for his first attacking shot, edged one which bounced higher than he had expected. Nor did Gatting, intent only on playing for stumps, survive with complete ease, all of which emphasized the quality of Broad's innings. He was 146 not out at the end of the day, and pink with smiling glory.

The second day of the match was eventually dominated by the stand between Gower and Richards, but Australia had a good start with Gatting slicing a drive into the gully, Broad touching Reid to a diving Zoehrer and Botham edging a ball angled across him to second slip.

All this might have been quite serious for England had not Gower been in a dominating mood from the outset of his innings. There was a streaky shot or two as he raced to 50 half an hour before lunch with nine fours, but the majority of his runs came from searing cuts, drives and hooks and after a dizzy morning in which England had garnered 107 for three off only 27 overs, Gower's score stood at 70 not out. It was a joy to watch him playing so well again and to see him smiling at the end of the day not out of stoicism, as so often he was obliged to do during the 11 wearying Tests which preceded this series, but out of justifiable pleasure that he had again been able to draw out the full richness of his natural gifts.

Yet, remarkably enough, Gower spent much of the afternoon in a Cornish shadow. Richards, 13 not out at lunch, played with quite extraordinary confidence and panache. A memorable stroke off his legs, no more than feathered to the square-leg boundary, brought up England's 400, and six other boundaries studded Richards's first Test 50, scored in a mere 94 minutes. Gower reached his 14th Test hundred for England before tea but Richards, making the most of (a) the pitch, (b) the innocuous bowling and (c) the lion's share of the strike, made 75 in the

afternoon session and proceeded to his first Test hundred without, it seemed, a moment's doubt.

Gower gave a chance to first slip when 113 which the wicket-keeper intercepted and missed, but the stand had reached 207, just short of the record for the sixth wicket against Australia, jointly held by Hutton and Hardstaff in 1938 and Boycott and Knott in 1977, when Greg Matthews had Gower caught at cover, his only wicket in the match.

England declared when Richards skied to long-off and during half an hour's batting at the end of the day, Boon played onto his stumps, hurried for pace by the much-improved Dilley.

Australia did well to reply to England's daunting total by batting until after lunch on the fourth afternoon. They were under pressure against attacking fields for much of Sunday, when England toiled diligently for a further five wickets on a still near-perfect wicket. Emburey, less at home in the cross breezes than many a previous English off-spinner (part of his skill is to make the ball drift and curve on still days, too) did not bowl at his best but Edmonds did, getting Ritchie with a snorter and Jones with the help of a fine low catch at backward short-leg by Athey. The best catch, however, on a day in which England's fielding looked snappy throughout, was held a few yards further back in the same position where Broad clung on to a firm hook by Marsh to give Botham one of his luckiest wickets.

Botham also got into the act with three slip catches, the third of them a beauty to dismiss the pugnacious Greg Matthews. But England took a long time to dismiss Waugh, who justified his promotion to number three with an innings of flair, and they had to wait until the follow-on had finally been saved before they got the most important wicket of all.

An old-fashioned wicket. Phil Edmonds gets a ball to bite and turn – one of the few that did so on Perth's adamantine pitch – to have an unlucky Ritchie caught at slip by Botham.

Dean Jones caught by Athey off Edmonds at short-leg in the first innings. The umpire is Dick French, though all eyes seem to be on his colleague.

Allan Border's innings saved the follow-on and, effectively, the match as well. Here he sweeps Emburey off his stumps against the spin, a ploy he used effectively against the England spinners throughout the series.

Allan Border was at his dedicated best as he scored his 20th Test hundred. He broke Emburey's spell by sweeping him whenever possible, and cutting him firmly if ever he pitched short and wide. Most of his runs, however, came from decisive off and straight drives against DeFreitas or Botham whom Gatting used from the Swan River End where the breeze helped them to swing the ball away from the left-hander.

Eighty-one not out when the rest day came with Australia 309 for six, Border was still batting when, just before lunch on the fourth morning, accompanied by the admirable Reid, Emburey pitched short enough for him to hammer a four past cover and take the total to 393.

Dilley deservedly picked up two of the last four wickets, including that of Border himself, held at the second attempt off the outside edge, before England set about building as quickly as possible on their lead of 191.

As so often in these circumstances, the batting side found it hard to pace themselves right and only Gower, in another glorious display of cultured attacking batsmanship, and Gatting, in what was nearly a very good innings, got things right. Reid bowled beautifully again, his dangerous slow yorker accounting this time for Lamb; and Waugh, in a very steady and determined spell of medium-paced bowling, took a further opportunity to make himself indispensable to a team short of class players. With a day to go, England were 199 for eight, 390 ahead.

Gatting had decided against declaring half an hour before the end of the day, feeling England had not scored quite quickly enough to justify giving Australia even the slightest sniff of a target within range. But he did declare the following morning thus wasting the chance of finding out whether a further squashing with the heavy roller might have caused the huge cracks in the pitch to start crumbling. This smacked of indecision.

Steve Waugh's bowling was not to be underestimated. His long and steady spell in the second innings prevented Gatting from declaring as early as he would have liked – or, perhaps, as early as he *should*.

Boon was out to the first ball of the day from Dilley, which he edged to second slip, but in Dilley's next over Botham failed to gather a harder, lower chance – Marsh, then one, being the escapee – and by lunchtime the resolute West Australian, in company with a confident and assertive Jones, had taken the score to 81 without any further serious mishap. When he was 13 Jones was lucky to get the benefit of the doubt against Dilley, however, and, if Dilley had been fortunate to get Zoehrer leg-before earlier in the game, he was unlucky with more than one shout on the tense final day.

Gatting was too slow to get Emburey and Edmonds on in harness and opened after lunch with Dilley and Botham, instead of keeping the spinners on and giving himself a greater chance with the second new ball with fresher fast bowlers. Instead, two balls through his seventh over, Botham broke down with a pulled inter-costal muscle (between the ribs) and for a wasted period Gatting used DeFreitas and himself to containing fields as if he was seriously worried about Australia getting the runs. This had to be wrong. Indeed if Australia had become interested in victory it would only have increased England's chances of bowling them out.

It needed a run-out, from a direct hit on the stumps by Broad from mid-off, to revive English hopes and when Marsh and Border went shortly before, and immediately after tea, anything was still possible. But as Edmonds and Emburey hurried England through to the second new ball, Ritchie and Matthews kept their heads down and their bats straight and Australia completed their very important escape. Matthews took every opportunity he could to reduce the number of balls bowled to him. In other words, he wanted a lot of time!

Under his wing? Ian Botham took an avuncular interest in the rapid progress of Phillip DeFreitas, whom he saw as his likely successor.

Test cricket in Australia would have suffered a long-term blow had England gone two-up with three to play. A draw guaranteed bigger crowds at Adelaide than the poor gates at Brisbane and the modest ones at Perth.

AUSTRALIA v ENGLAND (Second Test)

Played at Perth on 28, 29, 30 November 2, 3 December 1986
Toss: England. Result: Match drawn. Man of the match: B.C. Broad

ENGLAND

B.C. Broad	c Zoehrer b Reid	162	lbw b Waugh		16
C.W.J. Athey	b Reid	96	c Border b Reid		6
A.J. Lamb	c Zoehrer b Reid	0	(4) lbw b Reid		2
*M.W. Gatting	c Waugh b C.D. Matthews	14	(3) b Waugh		70
D.I. Gower	c Waugh b G.R.J. Matthews	136	c Zoehrer b Waugh		48
I.T. Botham	c Border b Reid	0	c G.R.J. Matthews b Reid		6
†C.J. Richards	c Waugh b C.D. Matthews	133	c Lawson b Waugh		15
P.A.J. DeFreitas	lbw b C.D. Matthews	11	b Waugh		15
J.E. Emburey	not out	5	not out		4
P.H. Edmonds					
C.R. Dilley					
Extras	(b 4, lb 15, w 3, nb 13)	35	(b 4, lb 9, nb 4)		17
Total	8 wickets declared	**592**	8 wickets declared		**199**

AUSTRALIA

G.R. Marsh	c Broad b Botham	15	(2) lbw b Emburey		49
D.C. Boon	b Dilley	2	(1) c Botham b Dilley		0
S.R. Waugh	c Botham b Emburey	71			
D.M. Jones	c Athey b Edmonds	27	(3) run out		69
*A.R. Border	c Richards b Dilley	125	(4) c Lamb b Edmonds		16
G.M. Ritchie	c Botham b Edmonds	33	(5) not out		24
G.R.J. Matthews	c Botham b Dilley	45	(6) not out		14
†T.J. Zoehrer	lbw b Dilley	29			
G.F. Lawson	b DeFreitas	13			
C.D. Matthews	c Broad b Emburey	10			
B.A. Reid	not out	2			
Extras	(b9, lb 9, nb 11)	29	(b 9, lb 6, nb 10)		25
Total		**401**	4 wickets		197

AUSTRALIA	O	M	R	W	O	M	R	W
Lawson	41	8	126	0	9	1	44	0
C.D. Matthews	29.1	4	112	3	2	0	15	0
Reid	40	8	115	4	21	3	58	3
Waugh	24	4	90	0	21.3	4	69	5
G.R.J. Matthews	34	3	124	1				
Border	2	0	6	0				

ENGLAND	O	M	R	W	O	M	R	W
Botham	22	4	72	1	7.2	4	13	0
Dilley	24.4	4	79	4	15	1	53	1
Emburey	43	9	110	2	28	11	41	1
DeFreitas	24	4	67	1	13.4	2	47	0
Edmonds	21	4	55	2	27	13	25	1
Gatting					5	3	3	0
Lamb					1	1	0	0

FALL OF WICKETS

Wkt	E 1st	A 1st	E 2nd	A 2nd
1st	223	4	8	0
2nd	227	64	47	126
3rd	275	114	50	142
4th	333	128	123	152
5th	339	198	140	
6th	546	279	172	
7th	585	334	190	
8th	592	360	199	
9th		385		
10th		401		

Umpires: R.A. French and P.J. McConnell.

CHAPTER FIVE

STALEMATE AT ADELAIDE

One up with three to play, the England team had certainly missed an important chance to win at Perth and some of their number, notably Phil Edmonds, felt that they had not pressed hard enough for victory. In his words, 'None of us, including the captain, was anywhere near aggressive enough during the Australian last-day battle for survival. In retrospect I'm sure that because there were numerous cracks in the wicket, which had on a couple of occasions resulted in unplayable deliveries, a sense of inevitability spread through the side; a "sit back and wait" attitude...'

Nevertheless, England were now entering the most consistently successful period of their long tour, and they began it by defeating Victoria in the Sir Robert Menzies Memorial Match. It began with an embarrassment because Mike Gatting failed to wake up in time to toss the coin and lead his men onto the field on the opening day. More of this anon. Suffice to say for the moment that Gatting, having arrived on the ground 20 minutes after the start of the play, was soon in the thick of the action, taking four for 31 with his bustling medium-pacers, no fewer than three Victorian batsmen obligingly hooking long-hops to deep square-leg!

Small and Foster bowled really well in helpful conditions on a grey day, but no-one in the circumstances begrudged Gatting his eye-catching and face-saving figures. Moreover, his effort was significant in the light of the fact that it was by now becoming clear that Botham would not recover from his torn inter-costal muscle in time for the third Test in Adelaide.

A wide-awake Mike Gatting making up for time lost to sleep during his four for 31 stint against Victoria at Melbourne.

Botham was not the only one with pain in the region of the ribs because, during the course of a plucky and accomplished innings of 58, Bruce French was hit in the chest by a ball from Mervyn Hughes. He played for the rest of the match but a chest infection, thought eventually to have been a virus aggravated by depression and the bruising caused by the ball from Hughes, caused him to spend most of the subsequent match in hospital. The second innings at Melbourne was notable for another fine piece of bowling by Small, and an unlucky one by Foster; then came rare opportunities for Slack and Whitaker to show what they were capable of.

VICTORIA v ENGLAND XI

Played at Melbourne on 6, 7, 8, 9 December 1986
Toss: Victoria. Result: England XI won by five wickets

VICTORIA

D.F. Whatmore	c French b Small	4		c and b Small	43
I.D. Frazer	lbw b Foster	0	(7)	c Richards b Small	10
D.M. Jones	c Lamb b Foster	4		c Richards b Small	29
P.A. Hibbert	c French b Foster	25		c Gower b Edmonds	91
J.D. Siddons	c Foster b Gatting	7		c sub (P.A.J. DeFreitas) b Small	3
S.P. O'Donnell	c Foster b Gatting	4		st Richards b Edmonds	77
A.I.C. Dodemaide	c Foster b Gatting	6	(2)	lbw b Small	24
†M.G.D. Dimattina	not out	19		c Lamb b Foster	20
M.G. Hughes	c Gower b Gatting	17		b Foster	20
*R.J. Bright	c French b Small	0		lbw b Foster	1
S.P. Davis	b Small	2		not out	0
Extras	(b 1, lb 3, w 1, nb 8)	13		(b 9, lb 8, nb 10)	27
Total		**101**			**345**

ENGLAND XI

W.N. Slack	c sub (G.L. Jordan) b Hughes	10		c Dimattina b O'Donnell	35
C.W.J. Athey	c Hibbert b Hughes	58		c Dimattina b Dodemaide	10
J.J. Whitaker	c Frazer b Hughes	0		c Whatmore b Bright	48
D.I. Gower	c Dimattina b O'Donnell	23	(5)	not out	28
C.J. Richards	c Dodemaide b O'Donnell	0	(7)	not out	0
*M.W. Gatting	c Whatmore b Dodemaide	1		b Dodemaide	17
†B.N. French	c Whatmore b Dodemaide	58			
A.J. Lamb	c sub (G.L. Jordan) b Dodemaide	46	(4)	c Jones b Bright	36
P.H. Edmonds	c Dimattina b Dodemaide	0			
N.A. Foster	not out	46			
G.C. Small	c Dodemaide b Bright	3			
Extras	(b 10, lb 6, w 1, nb 1)	18		(lb 1, w 8, nb 1)	10
Total		**263**		**5 wickets**	**184**

ENGLAND XI	O	M	R	W	O	M	R	W	FALL OF WICKETS				
										V	E	V	E
Small	15	3	30	3	40	9	81	5	*Wkt*	*1st*	*1st*	*2nd*	*2nd*
Foster	15	6	29	3	42.1	9	115	3	1st	7	28	60	14
Gatting	14	4	31	4	24	6	57	0	2nd	7	30	106	88
Edmonds	8	5	7	0	25	5	50	2	3rd	16	58	107	112
Athey					4	0	25	0	4th	33	78	112	140
									5th	37	83	239	180
VICTORIA	O	M	R	W	O	M	R	W	6th	55	128	263	
Hughes	18	6	76	3	8	0	24	0	7th	63	193	308	
Davis	1	0	1	0					8th	91	199	342	
Dodemaide	23	6	76	4	12	2	46	2	9th	92	238	344	
O'Donnell	22	4	78	2	12.1	3	36	1	10th	101	263	345	
Bright	4.5	1	16	1	10	1	54	2					
Jones					3	2	23	0					

In the Victoria 2nd innings C.J. Richards kept wicket from 56/0 to 296/6.
Umpires: R.C. Bailhache and D.W. Holt.

Needing 184 to win in 46 overs before a paltry crowd whose every word echoed round the vast concrete stadium, England won with five wickets, two overs and five balls to spare thanks to a steady 35 by Slack, 36 by a carefree Lamb and 48 by Whitaker who, apart from some injudicious hooking, played some strokes of real flair. As one had predicted, they were enough to earn him his first Test cap.

The tension so evident in the England camp before the first Test in Brisbane returned as the team prepared for what seemed likely to be a crucial third match in Adelaide. If Australia did not win here, they would need to take both the last two Tests to regain the Ashes, but because of the injury to Ian Botham and the small cloud which blew up over Mike Gatting's head at the start of the win against Victoria, there seemed to be almost as much pressure on England not to lose as there was on Australia to win.

The affair of 'Rip Van Gatting' is perhaps best viewed from an Australian point. The balanced judgement of one of Australia's better, and senior cricket writers, Alan Shiell, was: 'If it weren't so funny and inconsequential, it would be serious.'

That his oversleeping was more of an embarrassment than a disgrace was partly because Gatting's failure to appear on time was quite uncharacteristic. He is not the only captain of an international side to have taken the field less than fresh, and of some characters stories still abound. But the unpalatable truth is that Test cricketers now have to operate under the intense scrutiny of the modern media and there was a certain irony in the fact that David Gower, who lost the captaincy soon after the tour of the West Indies partly because of his excessively 'laid-back' approach on that tour, should have been the man who was on hand, spick and span, to toss the coin and lead England into the field.

Sadly, the manager did not help by first attempting a well-intentioned but naive 'cover-up', then issuing a belated reprimand. An honest statement of the facts after they had been established, rather than an initially equivocal one about the captain being 'indisposed', followed by a voluntary fine for the skipper for turning up late, might have been the wisest way to bury the affair at birth.

The Test match pitch looked a beauty to bat on, even before the match began, despite interruptions in its preparation when a near-cyclone ripped part of the roofing off one of the stands. It was evenly grassed, hard and well rolled, and the groundsman, Les Burdett, ensured that it was dry when the match was started.

Both Foster and Small had bowled well in Melbourne, but England, for whom a draw would be no bad result given their one-nil lead and the expectation of 'result' pitches to come at Melbourne and Sydney, decided to go for the extra batsman, 24-year-old James Whitaker. Though it was asking a lot of Gatting to operate as the third seamer and stock bowler, especially as Dilley and DeFreitas were by no means an established new-ball pair, the odds were that Edmonds and Emburey would be doing much of the bowling anyway, and so it proved. On a pitch even closer to perfection than the one at the WACA, neither side possessed the depth or quality of bowling to get the other one out twice and even the West Indians might have struggled to do so.

There were four individual hundreds of which Broad's was the most important for his side, Boon's the most significant for his own career, Border's the most predictable and Gatting's by some way the most brilliant. He savaged Matthews and, to a lesser extent, Sleep in a three-hour innings of almost disdainful confidence.

Gatting's assertiveness and another steady and untroubled opening stand by Broad and Athey meant that England were never in any serious danger of having to follow on. This made the last two days a test of everybody's patience, and the overall crowd of under 45,000 was only just more than a quarter of Adelaide's record attendance figure in 1932–33.

There is an 11,000 waiting list for membership of the SACA but the public turned up in smaller numbers than they did for the limited-overs games at the end of January. The trend is the same throughout Australia, and has been so, of course, for many years now. Surprisingly, this was only the fourth draw in 24 Tests between Australia and England at Australia's

prettiest and most charming Test ground, but unusually chilly weather and the expectation of a draw from an early stage of the game made this, unfortunately, an easily forgettable Test match.

As far as batting first was concerned, the boot was this time on the other foot as Australia, by winning an important toss, had first use of the lovely batting conditions. In the absence of Botham, with his torn side, Gatting must have wished for a third seamer as early as half an hour into the first morning. Dilley, having started with a perfectly pitched late outswinger – unfortunately for him to Marsh, not Boon – soon realized there was nothing in the pitch for him and DeFreitas, overstepping frequently from the River

Marsh and Boon. Their hitherto very successful opening partnership had been born almost exactly a year before in the Adelaide Test against India. They celebrated the anniversary with an opening stand of 113.

Torrens end, also had to settle for bowling well below his fastest pace. But so good was the wicket that neither Botham, nursing his injury in the pavilion, nor the two reserve fast bowlers, Small and Foster, would have done much to disturb the rapidly increasing peace of mind of the two Australian openers.

Marsh was, as usual, calm as Lake Eyre and solid as Ayer's Rock. Boon meanwhile, badly in need of runs, set about making them with admirable, orthodox batting. Whenever the two fast bowlers strayed to the legside of middle, he punched them away through mid-wicket with a decisive thrust of powerful wrists and forearms.

By teatime it was clear enough that the limit of England's ambition would have to be a draw and that the bulk of their bowling would be done by Edmonds and Emburey. Both, and especially Edmonds, bowled with immaculate control and skilful changes of pace and trajectory. Their only wicket by tea was that of Marsh, unluckily bowled off his body as he swung to leg, having occupied the crease for another 196 minutes, taking his total batting time against England to 1,668 minutes in seven innings. But on this occasion he had been too cautious for the good of a side batting on so perfect a pitch and one down in the series.

Sixty-five not out at tea, Boon produced a flurry of good shots after the interval, hooking, off-driving and on-driving Dilley for four fours in two overs. His fourth Test hundred and his second in a year at Adelaide was reached with a rasping cover-drive, but he and Jones were tied down by the spinners, with some useful help by Gatting, who conceded only 13 in a seven-over spell. In his only deliberate attempt to loft the ball, Boon had the misfortune to thump the ball very hard but straight into James Whitaker's

solar plexus, Whitaker clinging on as if the future of his watching father's chocolate business depended on it.

Because their slow bowlers were much the steadier, England had bowled 92 overs by the end of a day when the required minimum was cut down to 85 because of two brief interruptions for morning showers. Australia's 207 for two insured them, more or less, from defeat, perhaps, but it was too few runs on such a wicket. They made up for lost time on the second day, adding a further 307 in only 79 overs, due partly to some attractive batting by Border and Jones in the first session and partly to a brilliant yet measured assault by Waugh who, in company with Matthews, added 49 off four overs before the declaration. Border gave himself out caught off the glove in the last over before lunch after batting with style and comfort. It was a very important wicket for Edmonds to have taken because it enabled Gatting to retain a measure of control. Jones followed him soon after lunch, well held down the legside by Richards, a wicket which encouraged Dilley to keep going steadily at an important time.

Jones had moved his feet well to the spinners and all the Australian batsmen were able to have a comfortable long look at the England spinners, a fact which can only have increased their confidence against them for battles on more difficult pitches later in the series.

Ritchie, after playing in his usual effortless way, tried to hit DeFreitas over mid-on and sliced to mid-off, but this was England's last success because Matthews, after a long reconnaissance, also used his feet well to punch anything short through the covers whilst Waugh, in a situation which allowed him to give free rein to his immense natural ability, drove, pulled and cut with a marvellous panache. One cover drive, played through extra cover on bended knee, was like a photograph of Walter Hammond.

Australia thus took the field in high spirits, leaving themselves half an hour's bowling. It quickly became apparent, however, that Broad and Athey, tired though they may have been, were unlikely to miss out on the fun of batting on a pitch like this. In eight overs, two of them by the leg-spinner, Sleep, they made 29 and proceeded the following morning towards a comfortable hundred partnership.

Athey cut a leg-break from Sleep onto his off-stump in the 37th over but Broad, surviving a sticky period against Hughes just before lunch, proceeded to a stately hundred, his second in consecutive Tests.

Chris Broad at full stretch to kill the bounce during his second hundred in successive Tests.

The outstanding innings, however, was played by Gatting. One had backed him to respond positively and decisively to his embarrassing day the previous Saturday when he had set so poor an example by oversleeping, and so he did. Having made a brisk nine in five minutes before lunch, Gatting launched himself into Matthews in the afternoon. Sauntering down the pitch to loft him over mid-on, he pulled two more savage fours in the same over, and then climbed into Sleep's leg-spin with equal confidence, though the stocky Sleep, playing in his fifth Test match after a four-year gap, was much the more threatening of the two spinners.

Gatting's seventh Test hundred came from only 140 balls and was no doubt the easiest he has made. Nevertheless, it was a performance of almost Napoleonic authority. He made 91 out of a stand of 161 with Broad, who once again relied on a straight bat and rigid concentration. He fell to the first cross-bat shot he played, a firm pull which was bravely caught by Marsh at mid-wicket.

With the new ball due, and Lamb in need of runs after a long, barren spell in Test cricket, the question now seemed to be whether Gatting could get to his 100 before Border called back his faster bowlers. Waugh, given a belated spell, was as tidy as anyone and Sleep, too, was persevering manfully but Gatting danced down the pitch to thump a high-flighted ball over mid-on for his 15th four and his third Test hundred against Australia before hauling the next ball, which turned more than he expected, straight to mid-wicket.

Gatting must have kicked himself hard when he got back to the dressing-room because this left Lamb and Gower with an awkward last hour to bat and neither survived it. Gower, in one of his careless moods, was dropped at slip by Boon off Waugh when only nine and Lamb

Gatting's hundred was 'by some way the most brilliant innings in the match'. Here he dispatches Matthews crisply to the invitingly short square boundary, ignoring the close attentions of Waugh and Marsh.

never got going. Even on so good a wicket as this it was clear that with his increasingly 'square-on' technique he would be vulnerable to the new ball and, when it was taken with half an hour to go, he played a shot which will give him nightmares and which presented Hughes with a wicket he deserved after some hostile fast bowling.

One over later, after Emburey had come in as night-watchman, Whitaker's entry could be delayed no longer because Reid had Gower leg before, missing a drive.

England's last five wickets could add only 106 more runs on the fourth day but in doing so they occupied the crease long enough to insure themselves against defeat. Whitaker was, it must be frankly admitted, a disappointment. He looked vulnerable against Reid because he would not, like so many of his colleagues, get his back foot across to counteract the angle of Reid's attack. His method, which is to hit the ball 'inside out', makes him particularly susceptible to balls moving away towards the slips. In addition, like Lamb, he tends to push the bat out well in front of his body, making him also a 'caught and bowled' candidate and, to continue to be devil's advocate, he is apparently an impulsive hooker. On the credit side is his wonderful gift of timing. This, I am sure, will get him his Test hundreds in due course, but, when he had made 11, he was first dropped at second slip off Reid and then, next ball, top-edged an intended pull to mid-wicket and was caught at mid-off. Four of England's top six batsmen had by now been out to the same shot.

The shrewd and single-minded Emburey was not going to try anything flamboyant against the quick stuff – and Hughes and Reid had him pinned back in defence. But when Sleep returned, Emburey frustrated him with two of his falling sweep shots, played in front of square as if his feet were tied together.

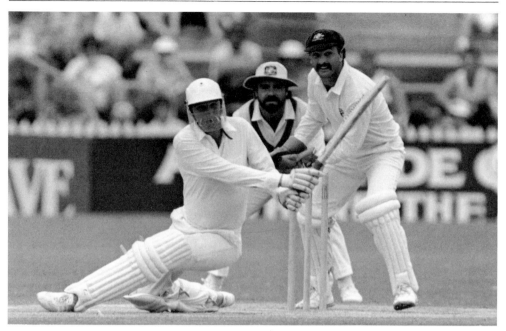

An Emburey exclusive, with apologies to Rohan Kanhai! The England vice-captain swept Sleep as if his feet were tied together. His innings, like this shot, was effective if unbeautiful. The wicket-keeper, Greg Dyer, looked a neat performer as stand-in for the more ebullient and noisy Tim Zoehrer.

Man of the match. Allan Border looked almost impossible to get out on the flawless pitch at Adelaide, scoring 70 in the first innings and 100 not out in the second.

James Whitaker during his brief hour of glory, a sparkling
century at the Adelaide Oval. Four years before he had sat
on the bank and vowed to play for England there one day.

An authentic Test opener. 'Swampy' Marsh taking evasive
action at Adelaide where he and Boon had their only
substantial stand.

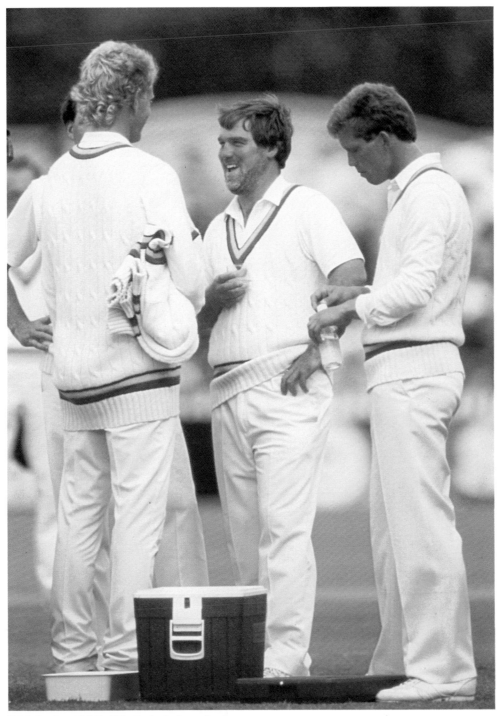

Drinks break at Adelaide. Mike Gatting looks as relaxed
and cheerful as he might be at the bar of his local in Enfield.

Cricket at close quarters. Greg Matthews, looking for quick
runs, has the attentive company of Jack Richards, John
Emburey (leg-slip) and Allan Lamb as he faces Phil Edmonds
during Australia's biggest total of the series at Adelaide.

Four more! Mike Gatting was brutal towards Greg
Matthews during his authoritative hundred in the third
Test. Geoff Marsh (left) and Greg Dyer would agree.

England's Player of the Season! Chris Broad thumps a four off the back foot during the third match of the rubber when he made the second of his three hundreds in successive Tests.

Then, having moved the fielder in front of square, he played an orthodox sweep for a third four: canny professionalism.

Richards played rather more orthodox cricket and, although the Reid/ Sleep combination eventually accounted for both the eighth-wicket pair and for Edmonds and Dilley too, Australia found it hard work building on their lead of 59.

Dilley and DeFreitas, at opposite ends to those from which they had bowled in the first innings, looked a much more hostile pair of opening bowlers. Boon was lbw at the third time of asking and Jones was caught fending a nasty lifter off his face. But Marsh once more showed his quality, batting for more than two hours, for much of this time in company with Border, who tried hard to dominate the spinners. But, with the ball now turning, Border needed some luck to be 31 not out at the close, with the Australian lead now 141 and seven wickets left.

The final day was dull, not helped by the loss of 12 overs in the morning due to showers. This reduced the options open to Border, who batted through until tea with Ritchie, reaching his 21st century for Australia, his seventh against England and his ninth since becoming captain, a quite remarkable achievement. Only when sweeping against the spinners did he look to be in any danger of getting out, although he deliberately used the shot to frustrate them and generally chose the right length. His judgement and concentration were, as usual, impeccable. Ritchie was never in trouble and made nonsense of suggestions that he should be dropped.

Left with a possible two hours to bat, England lost Athey, caught down the leg-side from a hook, and Gatting, bowled first ball trying to hit Matthews against the spin. As a result, Border could claim to have ended the match with the upper hand, and he won the man of the match award

himself, but England were quite satisfied with their draw in the absence of the injured Botham.

Peter Sleep in action on his home ground. The South Australian leg-spinner justified his selection after a four-year absence with some long and tidy spells.

AUSTRALIA v ENGLAND (Third Test)

Played at Adelaide on 12, 13, 14, 15, 16 December 1986
Toss: Australia. Result: Match drawn. Man of the match: A.R. Border

AUSTRALIA

G.R. Marsh	b Edmonds	43	(2) c and b Edmonds		41
D.C. Boon	c Whitaker b Emburey	103	(1) lbw b DeFreitas		0
D.M. Jones	c Richards b Dilley	93	c and b Dilley		2
*A.R. Border	c Richards b Edmonds	70	not out		100
G.M. Ritchie	c Broad b DeFreitas	36	not out		46
G.R.J. Matthews	not out	73			
S.R. Waugh	not out	79			
P.R. Sleep					
†G.C. Dyer					
M.G. Hughes					
B.A. Reid					
Extras	(lb 2, nb 15)	17	(b 4, lb 6, nb 2)		12
Total	5 wickets declared	514	3 wickets declared		201

ENGLAND

B.C. Broad	c Marsh b Waugh	116	not out		15
C.W.J. Athey	b Sleep	55	c Dyer b Hughes		12
*M.W. Gatting	c Waugh b Sleep	100	b Matthews		0
A.J. Lamb	c Matthews b Waugh	14	not out		9
D.I. Gower	lbw b Reid	38			
J.E. Emburey	c Dyer b Reid	49			
J.J. Whitaker	c Matthews b Reid	11			
†C.J. Richards	c Jones b Sleep	29			
P.A.J. DeFreitas	not out	4			
P.H. Edmonds	c Border b Sleep	13			
G.R. Dilley	b Reid	0			
Extras	(b 4, lb 14, w 4, nb 4)	26	(b 2, lb 1)		3
Total		455	2 wickets		39

ENGLAND XI	O	M	R	W	O	M	R	W
Dilley	32	3	111	1	21	8	38	1
DeFreitas	32	4	128	1	16	5	36	1
Emburey	46	11	117	1	22	6	50	0
Edmonds	52	14	134	2	29	7	63	1
Gatting	9	1	22	0	2	1	4	0

AUSTRALIA	O	M	R	W	O	M	R	W
Hughes	30	8	82	1	7	2	16	1
Reid	28.4	8	64	4				
Sleep	47	14	132	4	5	5	0	0
Matthews	23	1	102	0	8	4	10	1
Waugh	19	4	56	1	3	1	10	0
Border	1	0	1	0				

FALL OF WICKETS

	A	E	A	E
Wkt	1st	1st	2nd	2nd
1st	113	112	1	21
2nd	185	273	8	22
3rd	311	283	77	
4th	333	341		
5th	368	341		
6th		361		
7th		422		
8th		439		
9th		454		
10th		455		

Umpires: A.R. Crafter and S.G. Randell.

CHAPTER SIX
HAPPY CHRISTMAS

I t was a relief to arrive in Tasmania after the hitherto hectic and unrelenting pace of the tour. To open the window at the Wrest Point Hotel in Hobart and look out on the peaceful, albeit grey, waters of the Derwent River was a delightful contrast after the plush but noisy hotels in the centre of Australia's other major cities. Here one really might have been in Scotland or, since we were on the Derwent, the Lake District, and just to complete the sudden feeling of being in a home from home, it was pouring with rain when we all arrived after a delayed and pretty bouncy flight from Adelaide, as Australia's unusually unsummery summer continued.

Tasmania, especially Hobart in the south, has never been renowned for hot weather and when the Indians stayed there for their match at the same time the previous year, not a ball was bowled over the four days. This time the residue of recent heavy rain caused the first day to be totally abandoned, which not only gave everyone a welcome break but also eventually enabled England to win, well inside three days, with Foster, DeFreitas and Small – who bowled a heroic 14-over spell in a strong gale – whipping Tasmania out for 79 on a drying pitch in the first innings.

The TCA ground at Hobart is a sad case of missed opportunity. Scenically it is one of the most beautiful cricket grounds anywhere in the world with the broad estuary of the Derwent on one side and Mount Wellington on the other; but, partly because of local politics and the struggle for supremacy in cricket circles

between North and South Tasmania, the ground's potential has never been fulfilled. Modern stands would have given some protection from the elements and, if tastefully designed, might still have kept the physical beauties of the place intact. Instead, however, development is going to be made to another Hobart ground, the Bellerive Oval, where Test cricket is planned before the end of the decade.

England's batting performance against a Tasmanian attack which included Richard Ellison, who was enjoying a useful recuperative season on the island, and Steve Milosz, a useful leg-spinner of Hungarian parentage, was possibly their best of the tour against a State side. Its happiest features were a fine, patient innings by the likeable and unfortunate Wilf Slack, and a remarkable piece of hitting by John Emburey, whose 46 comprised ten fours and a magnificent straight six off Milosz; it was the highest all-boundary innings yet recorded in first-class cricket.

Despite some resistance from the saturnine David Boon, aided by Kim Hughes's younger brother, Glenn, England wrapped up a confident innings victory midway through the afternoon of the third day's play.

The next stop was Canberra where Bob Hawke entertained the team at a convivial reception before seeing his personally selected team defeated in a one-day match before a large crowd on a sunny day. The chief cricketing interest lay in Ian Botham's performance and, despite continuing soreness in the ribs, he batted and bowled vigorously enough to assuage any fears about his fitness for the decisive Melbourne Test.

TASMANIA v ENGLAND XI

Played at Hobart on 18 (no play), 19, 20, 21 December 1986
Toss: England XI. Result: England XI won by an innings and 96 runs

TASMANIA

Player	Dismissal	Runs		Runs
E.J. Harris	c Athey b Small	14	(2) b Gatting	12
P.D. Bowler	lbw b DeFreitas	7	(1) run out	1
K. Bradshaw	c Lamb b Foster	7	c Slack b Foster	4
G.A. Hughes	lbw b Foster	0	lbw b DeFreitas	24
*D.C. Boon	c Broad b Foster	2	(6) c Emburey b Gatting	29
D.J. Buckingham	c Richards b Foster	0	(7) not out	43
†R.E. Soule	c Slack b Small	1	(5) lbw b Gatting	21
R.M. Ellison	c Richards b DeFreitas	13	c Richards b Small	5
T.J. Cooley	c Athey b DeFreitas	16	(10) b DeFreitas	3
R.L. Brown	c Richards b DeFreitas	9	(9) c Lamb b Small	6
S.J. Milosz	not out	0	b Small	1
Extras	(b 1, lb 1, nb 8)	10	(b 4, lb 8, w 4, nb 2)	18
Total		79		167

ENGLAND XI

Player	Dismissal	Runs
B.C. Broad	c Milosz b Cooley	15
W.N. Slack	c Ellison b Brown	89
J.J. Whitaker	c Soule b Ellison	37
A.J. Lamb	c Buckingham b Ellison	19
†C.J. Richards	lbw b Milosz	18
P.A.J. DeFreitas	c Bradshaw b Milosz	3
C.W.J. Athey	not out	30
*M.W. Gatting	b Cooley	30
J.E. Emburey	c Buckingham b Milosz	46
N.A. Foster	c and b Brown	25
G.C. Small	not out	3
Extras	(b 3, lb 5, w 1, nb 18)	27
Total	9 wickets declared	342

ENGLAND XI	O	M	R	W	O	M	R	W
DeFreitas	14.2	4	44	4	8	0	30	2
Small	14	9	8	2	13.3	3	44	3
Foster	16	5	20	4	15	2	37	1
Emburey	3	2	4	0	3	2	4	0
Gatting	3	2	1	0	17	5	40	3

TASMANIA	O	M	R	W	O	M	R	W
Cooley	21	0	85	2				
Ellison	21..5	4	61	2				
Brown	19	6	65	2				
Milosz	31	8	104	3				
Bowler	2	0	19	0				

FALL OF WICKETS

	T	E	T
Wkt	1st	1st	2nd
1st	25	41	3
2nd	25	111	11
3rd	27	143	41
4th	33	187	53
5th	35	198	92
6th	36	198	111
7th	36	234	130
8th	63	294	136
9th	75	334	164
10th	79		167

Umpires: D.R. Gregg and S.G. Randell.

23 December
CANBERRA: England XI beat Prime Minister's XI by
four wickets. Prime Minister's XI 240/5 in 50 overs (G.A.
Bishop 49, M.R.J. Veletta 75, A.R. Border 41*); England XI
241/6 in 47.4 overs (B.C. Broad 47, D.I. Gower 68, I.T.
Botham 43)

Christmas in a hotel is never Christmas at
home, but under David Gower's auspices
as Chief Entertainments Officer (how are
the mighty fallen!) a genuinely good time
was had by all. Prior to the team's
traditional fancy-dress party, the gentlemen
(some of them are gentlemen!) of the Press
treated the players and their wives to a
hilarious one-act play based around a
sleeping Mike Gatting and the Ghosts of
Christmas Past (can't bat), Christmas
Present (can't bowl) and Christmas Future
(can't field). That such heresies could be
uttered in public underlined the excellent
relations between Gatting's team and the
journalists of both countries.

Christmas frolics. Dilley (top) wastes some precious bubbles, though pirate captain Gatting and convicts Phillippe and
Frances Edmonds seem unworried. Also (above) the Botham Bunnies! Left to right: Liam, Cathy with Rebecca, Ian, Sarah
and the family nanny, who travelled with them.

Loosening up. Gatting (left) took the right decision to put Australia in. Botham (right), recovered from his torn muscle, made the most of helpful conditions.

So to Boxing Day and the fourth Test in which England surged to an unassailable two-love lead in the series by thrashing Australia in three days through a mixture of poor batting and excellent English bowling and fielding. Mike Gatting thus joined the short list of those England captains who have retained the Ashes away from home. As with Mike Brearley, his predecessor as Middlesex captain, his triumph was diluted slightly by the fact that Australia, with several leading players in South Africa, were not at their strongest. But now, as then, Australia are by no means without talent.

A certain Allan Border was amongst the no-hopers defeated by Brearley's side in 1978–79 and in Marsh, Jones, Ritchie, Reid and Waugh, the beleaguered Border has some good players around him still. Overawed by Botham; harried by accurate England bowling; unable to get an early breakthrough when England batted; and deprived by their own selectors of Ritchie, who should obviously have played, they will look upon the 1986–87 Melbourne Test as a miserable experience.

For England, after their humiliation in the Caribbean earlier in the year, and a wretched home summer against India and New Zealand, this late taste of victory's fruit was sweet indeed. They were lucky to win the toss but held every chance in the field in both the brief Australian innings as well as batting just well enough on a by no means unplayable MCG pitch. Gladstone Small, called in on Boxing Day morning when Graham Dilley's knee injury looked unlikely to stand up to a long bowl, was their hero and when he went into a restaurant that evening after the first but one hopes not the last of his five-wicket hauls in Test cricket, accompanied by his attractive fiancée, he was accorded a standing ovation.

England had done a thoroughly professional job in bowling Australia out for 141 by tea-time on the first day after winning the toss on a hard, greenish pitch. Two hundred and fifty might have been somewhere nearer par in the conditions but, having been 83 for three at the end of an exhilarating morning's cricket before a crowd of heartening proportions, 58,203, Australia lost their last seven wickets for only 33 runs as Small, with an inspired piece of seam bowling, and Ian Botham, running in off only 12 paces and varying his pace cleverly, scythed through the middle order with almost embarrassing haste.

Jack Richards had a field day, capturing Border (top), cutting at Botham, McDermott (above) after a headlong dash to long leg and three other good catches.

Dean Jones, in a stylish and confident innings, was comfortably the highest scorer, but if there were two more important wickets than his they were those of Marsh and Border, the two men with the tightest techniques. Both fell to short balls from Botham, one hooking, the other cutting. The Botham 'hex' on Australia? It certainly seemed as though neither batsman would have played so rash a stroke against another bowler. But it was impossible not to admire Botham's determined and intelligent bowling in conditions which called on the bowlers to hit the pitch with the seam and wait for the batsman to edge the ball. In addition, of course, Botham had only recently recovered from his torn muscle under the ribs and was still unable to let himself go without pain.

Small richly deserved his five wickets, three of which were picked up in his first eight overs after lunch at a cost of nine runs. He bowled a tight off-stump line at a lively pace to celebrate his late call-up for the side in place of Graham Dilley. The latter's knee injury was a great disappointment to those who had hoped that he might at last make it through a full five-Test series. He is not robust enough to be a consistently successful Test bowler. He would, however, have been a dangerous customer in the mainly overcast conditions on the opening day.

England's first innings, which eventually gained them a lead of 208, owed

Gladstone Small's first five-wicket Test collection was richly deserved. Matthews was the last of his first innings victims, and Boon (right) the first of two more successes in the second innings.

an immense amount to Broad's third hundred in successive Ashes Tests. Herbert Sutcliffe made three hundreds in two matches at Sydney and Melbourne in 1924–25 (indeed, he scored three Test hundreds at Melbourne alone that season), but otherwise only Jack Hobbs, Walter Hammond and Bob Woolmer had previously scored three in three consecutive Ashes Tests for England.

Woolmer's record (he did not score any hundreds against any other country, oddly enough) was spoiled a little by 'failing' to make a hundred in the Centenary Test, which divided his three hundreds at The Oval in 1975 and the first two games of 1977. I wondered, as England found themselves batting after tea on Boxing Day, whether they might not collapse as quickly as Australia had done in the Centenary match, thus repeating the events of that unforgettable game at the MCG on the eve of the Packer Revolution. But, nearly 10 years on, Australia had no Dennis Lillee and, in Broad, England had a batsman who, rather like John Edrich, had absolutely no interest in history even as recent as the last ball bowled. His entire concentration was applied to the ball which lay ahead and by keeping his bat rigidly straight, and skilfully leaving anything lifting nastily around his off-stump, he slowly built another firm foundation for England.

Athey again gave Broad useful and solid support in an opening stand of 58 before Reid, who lacks the inswinger which would make him into a world-class bowler, had him leg-before on the back foot, the umpire judging that the ball had not bounced outside the leg-stump.

England began the second day comfortably placed at 95 for one, with Broad already past 50, and Gatting determined to help him overtake Australia. But the home bowlers, supported, sadly, by a much smaller crowd than on the first day – an undoubted reflection of their failure to convince the public that they were worth giving up a holiday to go and watch, although the simultaneous Davis Cup Final at nearby Kooyong was a great counter-attraction – battled hard to get their team back into the game. Broad and Gatting needed a good deal of luck to get through the first two hours without being parted; despite improved batting conditions they added only 68 runs, mainly against Reid, Hughes and Sleep. At 139, Gatting, then 28, should have been run out by yards after a hesitation, but Boon's throw was awry and Zoehrer failed to gather it despite having time in hand. The luck turned after lunch. Gatting hooked the first ball in the air to long-leg, and for a time thereafter Broad struggled as his momentous third hundred approached. He duly reached it, bestowed a modest but heartfelt smile on 26,151 of Melbourne's sports-mad public, played a few more confident strokes but then got an outside edge to the deserving Hughes and from that point England's batting initiative was lost.

Lamb at least and at last got some sort of score but he remained awfully vulnerable near the off-stump to Hughes and Reid. Gower decided to attack the excellent Sleep, who achieved much more turn than the England finger-spinners could get the following day, and enabled Matthews to take one of two excellent catches, this one running back at mid-on.

Botham played Sleep with admirable restraint, planning an assault on the new ball, but almost as soon as it was taken he edged a massive drive at McDermott, whereupon the Brisbane Bull, hitherto unimpressive, did well to knock over three more tail-enders. But Emburey, Edmonds and, not least, Small, extended the innings beyond six o'clock with some enterprising batting.

Agony and ecstasy. Allan Lamb has a slice of luck as the ball loops into open space, much to the chagrin of Border and Zoehrer. Botham was not so lucky, caught Zoehrer bowled McDermott.

Once or twice McDermott behaved a little like McEnroe, which did his reputation no good. He has had too much adulation too soon, but is basically a good sort of chap, and a very strong young fast bowler. He will emerge from his recent slough of despond.

Australia added to their own problems by earning themselves a very substantial fine for failing to bowl their 90 overs on time. Then, on the third day, they collapsed a second time. Only Marsh and Border, supported by the gifted but still immature Jones and by Waugh, made England work hard enough for their wickets. Border fell to the best of several good slip catches – Small taking the vital wicket – and Marsh, having been given not out when caught off his glove two balls earlier, much to England's grossly over-acted and almost rebellious display of chagrin, was run out by Edmonds. Once again Marsh had been admirable.

The Brisbane Bull. Craig McDermott played in only one Test, when he took four wickets, but he seemed too charged-up for his own good. With a cooler head he will undoubtedly come again for Australia.

Vain appeal. England's fielders, sniffing the Ashes, made an exaggerated fuss when Marsh was given not out for this catch by Athey, probably off his glove. Two balls later dismay turned to smiles when Marsh was run out.

The rest was an almost embarrassingly unequal 'struggle' between England's two merciless spinners and a feeble and demoralized Australian middle and lower order. The folly of leaving out Ritchie was all too evident. And to think that England had seriously contemplated leaving Edmonds out. He had a leading hand in both run-outs as well as taking three wickets. Would that there were two equally good spinners pressing Emburey and Edmonds for their places. But, for the moment there was no need to worry. In their present form and mood, England would have been a match for all Test teams except the West Indies, and they were very soon to prove that even *that* formidable team was no longer necessarily invincible.

Elton John shared in England's celebrations and got a few splashes on his beautiful velvet coat.

We also serve, who only stand and wait. The reserves enjoyed the victory and its fruits. Bruce French, Neil Foster and Wilf Slack drape James Whitaker with the Union Jack.

Drowned in beer – or is it champagne? The England captain won't let go of his Union Jack.

AUSTRALIA v ENGLAND (Fourth Test)

Played at Melbourne on 26, 27, 28 December 1986

Toss: England. Result: England won by an innings and 14 runs. Man of the match: G.C. Small

AUSTRALIA

G.R. Marsh	c Richards b Botham	17	(2) run out		60
D.C. Boon	c Botham b Small	7	(1) c Gatting b Small		8
D.M. Jones	c Gower b Small	59	c Gatting b DeFreitas		21
*A.R. Border	c Richards b Botham	15	c Emburey b Small		34
S.R. Waugh	c Botham b Small	10	b Edmonds		49
G.R.J. Matthews	c Botham b Small	14	b Emburey		0
P.R. Sleep	c Richards b Small	0	run out		6
†T.J. Zoehrer	b Botham	5	c Athey b Edmonds		1
C.J. McDermott	c Richards b Botham	0	b Emburey		1
M.G. Hughes	c Richards b Botham	2	c Small b Edmonds		8
B.A. Reid	not out	2	not out		0
Extras	(b 1, lb 1, w 1, nb 7)	10	(lb 3, w 1, nb 2)		6
Total		**141**			**194**

ENGLAND

B.C. Broad	c Zoehrer b Hughes	112
C.W.J. Athey	lbw b Reid	21
*M.W. Gatting	c Hughes b Reid	40
A.J. Lamb	c Zoehrer b Reid	43
D.I. Gower	c Matthews b Sleep	7
I.T. Botham	c Zoehrer b McDermott	29
†C.J. Richards	c Marsh b Reid	3
P.A.J. DeFreitas	c Matthews b McDermott	7
J.E. Emburey	c and b McDermott	22
P.H. Edmonds	lbw b McDermott	19
G.C. Small	not out	21
Extras	(b 6, lb 7, w 1, nb 11)	25
Total		**349**

ENGLAND XI	O	M	R	W	O	M	R	W
Small	22.4	7	48	5	15	3	40	2
DeFreitas	11	1	30	0	12	1	44	1
Emburey	4	0	16	0	20	5	43	2
Botham	16	4	41	5	7	1	19	0
Gatting	1	0	4	0				
Edmonds					19.4	5	45	3

AUSTRALIA	O	M	R	W
McDermott	26.5	4	83	4
Hughes	30	3	94	1
Reid	28	5	78	4
Waugh	8	4	16	0
Sleep	28	4	65	1

FALL OF WICKETS

Wkt	A 1st	E 1st	A 2nd
1st	16	58	13
2nd	44	163	48
3rd	80	198	113
4th	108	219	153
5th	118	251	153
6th	118	273	175
7th	129	277	180
8th	133	289	185
9th	137	319	189
10th	141	349	194

Umpires: R.A French and A.R. Crafter.

CHAPTER SEVEN

WINNERS AT THE WACA

For someone delighted to see England winning cricket matches again out of habit, yet convinced that too many tournaments like this one will only devalue further the currency of international cricket, it was impossible not to be ambivalent about England's sweeping victory in the Perth Challenge.

It was an outstandingly successful promotion, if judged in isolation from the remainder of the Australian season. The WACA is a splendid setting for cricket in its modernized form; the weather was hot and sunny throughout; the organization was slick and professional; the pitches were generally excellent; and five of the seven matches produced exciting finishes, a very high proportion. Crowds were large and profits high, despite generous prize-money, the lion's share of which was collected by Mike Gatting and his businesslike team. But this was, nonetheless, a superfluous competition, organized as part of a general Festival of Sport coinciding with the America's Cup, which is much more about big business and show business than it is about sport. Fortunes were being made, and a few more lost on the America's Cup. The very economy of Western Australia was heavily dependent on whether or not the challenging yacht was American. There would be far more big-spending Americans than there would be New Zealanders. Unfortunately for WA, the Americans under Dennis Connor not only challenged, they also conquered – and rather a one-sided affair the final group of races off Fremantle turned out to be.

The Perth Challenge cricket competition had been agreed to by overseas administrators anxious neither to offend PBL (Mr Packer's former marketing company) and the ACB, nor to miss any of the large profits still available in a land where patience has not yet, apparently, been lost by the public in limited-overs cricket, even when Australia are being beaten.

Those same administrators, from England, West Indies and Pakistan, were in Perth to enjoy the sunshine and to be 'wined and dined' by the home authority. Next stop was to be Sharjah in April for another four-nation competition. More profits; more easy money for the players. But who in the future would really care, or even remember, except those who were there, who won the Perth Challenge? And would it not render much less significant the World Cup, assuming it eventually took place, in India and Pakistan later in 1987?

This was not the fault, of course, of the players, although some of them might stop a moment to consider how quickly cricketing fortunes are won and lost in these days of hectic international competition. Because Australia is the world leader in the current over-indulgence, players seem to come and go here quicker than anywhere. Craig McDermott was a case in point: rushed into big-money matches too soon and apparently on the way to the scrapheap or perhaps South Africa – unless he was lucky.

England were quite clearly the outstanding team of the tournament. Having dealt with Australia, their key match was against the West Indies and they won it with a spirited, positive batting recovery, helped by over-defensive captaincy by Richards when England were in trouble at 96 for five after 25 overs.

Dean Jones was the outstanding batsman in the Perth Challenge. Here he drives Small during the first of successive hundreds against England and Pakistan.

Amongst some shaky West Indies batting, Gus Logie stood out. Michael Holding (below) was not so effective when he tried to hit Dilley out of the ground but instead skied a catch to Edmonds.

Australia's Player of the Season! Dean Jones shows Ian
Botham a raised left elbow and the full face of the bat
during his team's disastrous first innings at Melbourne.

The campfire is out; the wolves encircle their prey. Left to
right, Lamb, Athey, McDermott, Richards and Botham
during the latter stages of the decisive third day at
Melbourne.

The moment of victory! Bruce Reid walks towards the
pavilion after his partner Mervyn Hughes has been caught
by Gladstone Small at deep square-leg to complete
England's winning victory. Ian Botham celebrates mightily;
Jack Richards looks after the souvenirs.

The Ashes are ours! Jubilation for Gatting and Emburey.

Top: The WACA transformed from a windy open ground into a splendid modern stadium as it looked during the Australia v England match in the Perth Challenge.

Above: The executioner's axe! Botham getting a wide delivery during his 68 off 38 balls against Australia at Perth.

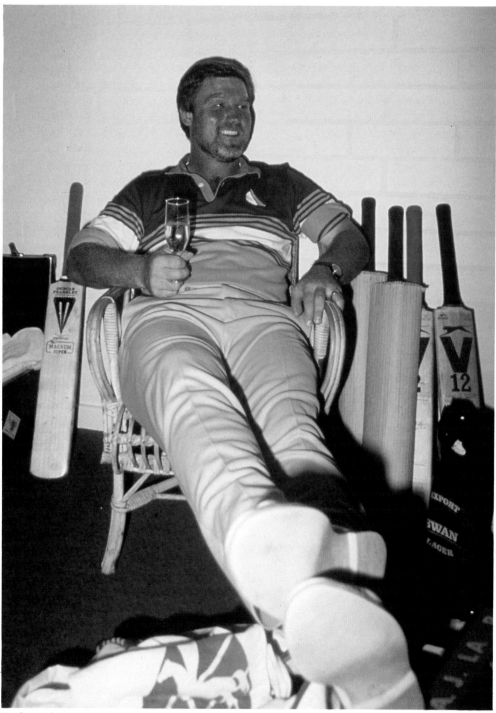

Trophy number two in the bag. As easy as shelling peas!

Against Australia Bill Athey put on 86 for the first wicket with Chris Broad before Botham produced one of his finest one-day innings for England.

The batting of Lamb (71) and Richards (50) gave Dilley, Small, Botham and the spinners something to work on and with the West Indies short of batting confidence after playing on bad pitches on their tour of Pakistan, England won a tense and genuinely absorbing game by 19 runs.

They had less trouble in the final, winning a valuable toss on a pitch being used for the fourth time. Dilley, DeFreitas, Small, Botham, Emburey and even Gatting all bowled well, eight catches were held and only 167 runs were required to make sure of the winners' cheque of £10,000.

Imran Khan and Wasim Akram are a formidable new-ball pair, and with the help of an umpiring error which accounted unjustly for Broad for the second time in successive innings, they had England apparently struggling at seven for two after four overs. But to watch England batting in Australia this winter was gradually to move from pessimism to optimism. Gower led the recovery, flashing and crashing to a quick 31 before unwisely trying to dominate Imran in his second spell instead of just seeing him off, whereupon Lamb, who returned to his best form during the four matches, led the deciding partnership of 89 with Gatting for the fourth wicket.

To win a final with as many as nine overs and five balls to spare with five wickets in hand was a very substantial achievement. But the true test of England's improvement during this tour would be measured by their ability to repeat their superiority over the West Indies during the long round of World Series internationals which followed the fifth Test.

PAKISTAN v WEST INDIES

Played at Perth on 30 December 1986
Toss: West Indies. Result: Pakistan won by 34 runs.
Man of the match: Mudassar Nazar

PAKISTAN

Qasim Omar	run out	30
Shoaib Mohammad	c Richards b Benjamin	34
Ramiz Raja	c Richardson b Gray	42
Javed Miandad	c Richards b Walsh	53
*Imran Khan	c Benjamin b Gray	16
Manzoor Elahi	c Richardson b Gray	4
Ijaz Ahmed	c sub (H.A. Gomes) b Gray	2
Wasim Akram	c Harper b Walsh	9
†Salim Yousuf	not out	2
Mudassar Nazar		
Salim Jaffer		
Extras	(lb 3, w 3, nb 1)	7
Total (50 overs)	8 wickets	**199**

WEST INDIES

C.G. Greenidge	b Akram	22
D.L. Hayes	c Yousuf b Mudassar	25
R.B. Richardson	run out	38
*I.V.A Richards	lbw b Mudassar	10
A.L. Logie	c Yousuf b Mudassar	7
†P.J.L. Dujon	c Shoaib b Jaffer	13
R.A. Harper	not out	20
W.K.M. Benjamin	c Jaffer b Shoaib	3
M.A. Holding	b Shoaib	5
A.H. Gray	c Imran b Jaffer	3
C.A. Walsh	b Akram	2
Extras	(lb 16, nb 1)	17
Total (46.2 overs)		**165**

BOWLING

WEST INDIES	O	M	R	W
Gray	10	1	45	4
Walsh	10	0	48	2
Holding	10	0	30	0
Benjamin	10	2	35	1
Harper	10	0	38	0
PAKISTAN				
Imran Khan	7	2	18	0
Salim Jaffer	10	2	29	2
Wasim Akram	7.2	2	13	2
Manzoor Elahi	2	0	10	0
Mudassar Nazar	10	0	36	3
Shoaib Mohammad	10	0	43	2

FALL OF WICKETS

	1	2	3	4	5	6	7	8	9	10
P	51	72	163	166	177	188	188	199		
WI	40	71	105	106	123	128	139	150	155	165

Umpires: S.G. Randell and P.J. McConnell.

AUSTRALIA v ENGLAND

Played at Perth on 1 January 1987
Toss: England. Result: England won by 37 runs.
Man of the match: I.T. Botham

ENGLAND

B.C. Broad	run out	76
C.W.J. Athey	c Zoehrer b O'Donnell	34
D.I. Gower	b Zoehrer b Whitney	6
A.J. Lamb	c Zoehrer b Reid	66
I. T. Botham	c Zoehrer b Waugh	68
*M.W.Gatting	not out	5
†C.J. Richards	c Border b Reid	4
P.A.J. DeFreitas	not out	0
J.E. Emburey		
G.C. Small		
G.R. Dilley		
Extras	(b 2, lb 6, w 4, nb 1)	13
Total (49 overs)	6 wickets	**272**

AUSTRALIA

G.R. Marsh	b Botham	28
D.C. Boon	c Embury b DeFreitas	1
D.M. Jones	c Gower b Dilley	104
*A.R. Border	b Emburey	26
S.R. Waugh	c Richards b Small	16
S.P. O'Donnell	run out	0
K.H. Macleay	c Emburey b Dilley	21
†T.J. Zoehrer	c Botham b DeFreitas	1
M.R. Whitney	run out	6
B.A. Reid	b DeFreitas	10
S.P. Davis	not out	1
Extras	(lb 7, w 10, nb 4)	21
Total (48.2 overs)		**235**

BOWLING

AUSTRALIA	O	M	R	W
Davis	8	1	48	0
Whitney	10	0	56	1
Macleay	9	0	51	0
Reid	10	1	46	2
O'Donnell	7	0	39	1
Waugh	5	0	24	1
ENGLAND				
DeFreitas	9.2	0	42	3
Dilley	10	1	31	2
Botham	10	0	52	1
Small	9	0	62	1
Emburey	10	0	41	1

FALL OF WICKETS

	1	2	3	4	5	6	7	8	9	10
E	86	95	150	256	262	271				
A	7	50	125	149	158	210	214	217	233	235

Umpires: R.A. French and P.J. McConnell.

AUSTRALIA v PAKISTAN

Played at Perth on 2 January, 1987
Toss: Australia. Result: Pakistan won by 1 wicket.
Man of the match: D.M. Jones

AUSTRALIA

G.R. Marsh	run out	28
G.A. Bishop	c Jaffer b Imran	6
D.M. Jones	b Akram	121
*A.R. Border	b Mudassar	14
S.R. Waugh	b Imran	82
G.R.J. Matthews	b Akram	3
S.P. O'Donnell	not out	9
K.H. Macleay	not out	1
†T.J. Zoehrer		
M.R. Whitney		
B.A. Reid		
Extras	(b 2, lb 1, w 5, nb 1)	9
Total (50 overs)	6 wickets	**273**

PAKISTAN

Qasim Omar	c Border b Waugh	67
Shoaib Mohammad	lbw b Macleay	9
Ramiz Raja	c Bishop b Macleay	0
Javed Miandad	b Reid	7
Mudassar Mazar	lbw b Waugh	7
*Imran Khan	c Zoehrer b Waugh	20
Manzoor Elahi	c and b Whitney	48
Asif Mujtaba	not out	60
†Salim Yousuf	c O'Donnell b Whitney	31
Wasim Akram	c Whitney b Waugh	5
Salim Jaffer	not out	3
Extras	(lb 15, w 1, nb 1)	17
Total (49.5 overs)	9 wickets	**274**

BOWLING

PAKISTAN	O	M	R	W
Imran Khan	10	0	43	2
Wasim Akram	10	1	58	2
Salim Jaffer	10	2	43	0
Mudassar Nazar	10	0	56	1
Asif Mujtaba	5	0	32	0
Shoaib Mohammad	3	0	22	0
Manzoor Elahi	2	0	16	0
AUSTRALIA				
Macleay	10	0	36	2
Whitney	10	0	58	2
Reid	10	0	61	1
Waugh	9.5	0	48	4
O'Donnell	10	0	56	0

FALL OF WICKETS

	1	2	3	4	5	6	7	8	9	10
E	26	49	70	243	254	271				
A	34	40	73	93	96	129	181	224	267	

Umpires: A.R. Crafter and S.G. Randell

ENGLAND v WEST INDIES

Played at Perth on 3 January 1987
Toss: West Indies. Result: England won by 19 runs.
Man of the match: G.R. Dilley

ENGLAND

B.C. Broad	c Garner b Marshall	0
C.W.J. Athey	c Richardson b Garner	1
D.I. Gower	c Dujon b Garner	11
A.J. Lamb	c Harper b Marshall	71
*M.W. Gatting	c Garner b Walsh	15
I.T. Botham	c Greenidge b Harper	11
†C.J. Richards	c Dujon b Garner	50
J.E. Emburey	c Harper b Garner	18
P.H. Edmonds	not out	16
G.R. Dilley	c and b Garner	1
G.C. Small	not out	8
Extras	(lb 10, w 8, nb 8)	26
Total (50 overs)	9 wickets	**228**

WEST INDIES

C.G. Greenidge	b Small	20
D.L. Haynes	lbw b Small	4
R.B. Richardson	c Gatting b Botham	12
*I.V.A. Richards	c Broad b Emburey	45
A.L. Logie	c Richards b Dilley	51
†P.J.L. Dujon	b Dilley	36
R.A. Harper	run out	4
M.D. Marshall	b Dilley	7
M.A. Holding	c Edmonds b Dilley	7
J. Garner	not out	4
C.A. Walsh	lbw b Emburey	0
Extras	(b 4, lb 9, w 4, nb 2)	19
Total (48.2 overs)		**209**

BOWLING

WEST INDIES	O	M	R	W
Marshall	10	1	30	2
Garner	10	0	47	5
Holding	10	0	33	0
Walsh	9	0	40	1
Harper	10	0	63	1
Richards	1	0	5	0
ENGLAND				
Dilley	10	0	46	4
Small	10	1	37	2
Botham	10	1	29	1
Edmonds	9	1	53	0
Emburey	9.2	0	31	2

FALL OF WICKETS

	1	2	3	4	5	6	7	8	9	10
E	3	10	35	67	96	156	194	209	211	
WI	9	39	51	104	178	187	187	201	208	209

Umpires: R.A. French and P.J. McConnell.

AUSTRALIA v WEST INDIES

Played at Perth on 4 January 1987
Toss: Australia. Result: West Indies won by 164 runs.
Man of the match: C.G. Greenidge

WEST INDIES

C.G. Greenidge	b Waugh	100
D.L. Haynes	c Zoehrer b Macleay	18
H.A. Gomes	b O'Donnell	18
*I.V.A. Richards	lbw b O'Donnell	13
A.L. Logie	b Reid	13
†P.J.L. Dujon	c Zoehrer b O'Donnell	9
R.A. Harper	c Zoehrer b O'Donnell	2
M.A. Holding	not out	53
J. Garner	lbw b McDermott	1
A.H. Gray	not out	10
C.A. Walsh		
Extras	(lb 13, w 3, nb 2)	18
Total (50 overs)	8 wickets	**255**

AUSTRALIA

D.C. Boon	b Garner	2
G.R. Marsh	c Richards b Gray	5
D.M. Jones	c Harper b Garner	2
*A.R. Border	c Greenidge b Holding	9
G.A. Bishop	c Dujon b Holding	7
S.R. Waugh	b Harper	29
S.P. O'Donnell	lbw b Harper	8
K.H. Macleay	c Logie b Holding	5
†T.J. Zoehrer	lbw b Gray	4
C.J. McDermott	c Gomes b Gray	7
B.A. Reid	not out	1
Extras	(lb 5, w 2, nb 5)	12
Total (35.4 overs)		**91**

BOWLING

AUSTRALIA	O	M	R	W
Reid	10	2	40	1
Macleay	10	1	29	1
McDermott	10	0	67	1
Waugh	10	0	41	1
O'Donnell	10	0	65	4
WEST INDIES				
Garner	6	2	10	2
Gray	7.4	0	9	3
Walsh	6	1	11	0
Holding	10	1	32	3
Harper	6	1	24	2

FALL OF WICKETS

	1	2	3	4	5	6	7	8	9	10
WI	46	95	127	176	176	180	203	210		
A	4	12	16	25	36	66	78	78	89	91

Umpires: A.R. Crafter and S.G. Randell.

ENGLAND v PAKISTAN

Played at Perth on 5 January 1987
Toss: Pakistan. Result: England won by 3 wickets.
Man of the match: B.C. Broad

PAKISTAN

Qasim Omar	b Botham	32
Shoaib Mohammad	c DeFreitas b Emburey	66
Ramiz Raja	run out	15
Javed Miandad	c Athey b Emburey	59
*Imran Khan	c Gower b DeFreitas	23
Manzoor Elahi	not out	9
Wasim Akram	not out	1
Asif Mujtaba		
†Salim Yousuf		
Mudassar Nazar		
Salim Jaffer		
Extras	(lb 15, w 1, nb 8)	24
Total (50 overs)	5 wickets	**229**

ENGLAND

B.C. Broad	c Yousuf b Imran	97
C.W.J. Athey	b Manzoor	42
D.I. Gower	c Shoaib b Mudassar	2
A.J. Lamb	c Javed b Shoaib	32
I.T. Botham	c Ramiz b Akram	10
*M.W. Gatting	run out	7
†C.J. Richards	run out	0
P.A.J. DeFreitas	not out	13
J.E. Emburey	not out	11
N.A. Foster		
G.C. Small		
Extras	(b 1, lb 13, w 3, nb 1)	18
Total (49.4 overs)	7 wickets	**232**

BOWLING

ENGLAND	O	M	R	W
DeFreitas	9	1	24	1
Small	10	0	41	0
Foster	4	0	23	0
Botham	10	1	37	1
Gatting	7	0	24	0
Emburey	10	0	65	2
PAKISTAN				
Wasim Akram	9.4	1	28	1
Salim Jaffer	10	2	43	0
Imran Khan	9	0	41	1
Mudassar Nazar	10	0	39	1
Asif Mujtaba	3	0	19	0
Manzoor Elahi	3	0	24	1
Shoaib Mohammad	5	0	24	1

FALL OF WICKETS

	1	2	3	4	5	6	7	8	9	10
P	61	98	156	198	225					
E	104	108	156	184	199	204	208			

Umpires: A.R Crafter and R.A. French.

ENGLAND v PAKISTAN (Final)

Played at Perth on 7 January 1987
Toss: England. Result: England won by 5 wickets.
Man of the match: Javed Miandad

PAKISTAN

Qasim Omar	c Broad b Botham	21
Shoaib Mohammad	b Dilley	0
Ramiz Raja	c Athey b Botham	22
Javed Miandad	not out	77
Asif Mujtaba	c Gower b Botham	7
*Imran Khan	c Richards b Gatting	5
Manzoor Elahi	c Gower b Small	20
†Salim Yousuf	c Athey b Small	0
Mudassar Nazar	c Gower b Emburey	0
Wasim Akram	c Gatting b Small	2
Salim Jaffer	not out	3
Extras	(lb 5, w 1, nb 3)	9
Total (50 overs)	9 wickets	**166**

ENGLAND

B.C. Broad	c Yousuf b Akram	0
C.W.J. Athey	c Yousuf b Imran	1
D.I. Gower	c Shoaib b Imran	31
A.J. Lamb	c Yousuf b Akram	47
*M.W. Gatting	b Akram	49
*I.T. Botham	not out	23
†C.J. Richards	not out	7
P.A.J. DeFreitas		
J.E. Emburey		
G.R. Dilley		
G.C. Small		
Extras	(lb 8, w 1)	9
Total (40.1 overs)	5 wickets	**167**

BOWLING

ENGLAND	O	M	R	W
DeFreitas	10	1	33	0
Dilley	10	0	23	1
Botham	10	2	29	3
Small	10	0	28	3
Emburey	8	0	34	1
Gatting	2	0	14	1
PAKISTAN				
Imran Khan	8	2	30	2
Wasim Akram	10	2	27	3
Salim Jaffer	10	1	43	0
Mudassar Nazar	5.1	0	22	0
Shoaib Mohammad	2	0	11	0
Manzoor Elahi	5	0	26	0

FALL OF WICKETS

	1	2	3	4	5	6	7	8	9	10
P	2	36	58	76	89	127	127	128	131	
E	1	7	47	136	145					

Umpires: A.R Crafter and R.A. French.

Graham Dilley (top) bowled superbly during the tournament. His early dismissal of Shoaib Mohammad set the pattern for the final, despite a masterly 77 by Javed Miandad (above).

England's all-too-noisy supporters (top) were in Seventh Heaven as the captain and his crew (above) sailed to victory in the America's Cup Challenge. Perth's weather was glorious throughout.

CHAPTER EIGHT

TAYLOR-MADE CONSOLATION

Australia's run of 14 Tests without a win, the longest in their history, although the time span was deceptively short (June 1985 to January 1987) came to a dramatic end when Peter Sleep bowled John Emburey with only one over of the fifth Test still to be played. It was Australia's third win in their last four Sydney Tests and in each case the main reasons for success were a pitch which took spin and a leg-spinner capable of exploiting it.

One of the most tense and evenly fought Ashes Tests produced a classic climax, with England starting the last day needing 281 to win with nine wickets left on a dry, tricky, but by no means lethal pitch on which Emburey had picked up his first seven-wicket haul in Tests the previous day.

It was difficult to believe that England had only once managed to score more than 300 to win a Test, one of the timeless games of the 1928–29 series. Then, on the seventh day, England prevailed by three wickets thanks largely to a partnership between Hobbs and Sutcliffe on a sticky wicket which has gone into the game's folklore. This time England lost Broad, 'man of the series' and the more dynamic half of the successful England opening partnership when only 24 of the 320 needed had been scored. But David Gower, coming in to join Bill Athey with half an hour left on the fourth evening stayed with him until 25 minutes before lunch on the last day. Then, two wickets with the score at 91 and a further two, in successive balls taken by the hitherto unknown Australian hero, Peter Taylor, in the first over after lunch, gave Australia their first definite scent of victory.

Indeed, when Botham spooned his first delivery from Taylor towards mid-wicket and saw Wellham sprinting in to hold a brilliant catch (thus ending his overseas Test career on a sad note) it seemed likely that we had seen the last of the game's marvellously unpredictable twists and turns. It was not so, however, because Gatting in a splendidly determined counter-attack against the spinners hurried to a powerfully punched 50 off only 68 balls, hitting seven fours and a six, enabling himself and Richards to take England into a position from which they could again think seriously about winning.

The Australian spin bowling was ordinary and Gatting brutally put away the plentiful supply of short balls so that, when the last 20 overs arrived at five o'clock, England needed only 90 more runs with five wickets in hand. But Gatting, cruelly denied his hundred by a fine stop by Wellham from a cracking square-cut, then pushed a return catch to Waugh. Richards, his cool and determined partner in a record England sixth-wicket stand at the SCG, was deceived by one of Sleep's rare googlies, whereupon Edmonds was given out first ball to a leg-break which hit his back leg close to the popping crease, though one was not certain if it had pitched on the stumps.

Small, Emburey and Dilley were left with nine overs and two balls to survive. Small was given out caught low at first slip with 14 balls to go and then Emburey went back to Sleep's final ball, a leg-break which crept a little. Deliriously happy Australians leapt into one another's arms in intense relief. If had been for them an unforgettable match with the totally unexpected selection of Taylor creating extra interest.

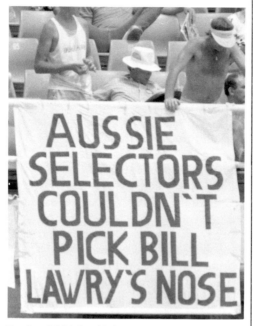

But they *did* pick Peter Taylor!

Considering the fact that the series had already been decided, it was something of a relief that the game was watched by more than 23,000 on both the first two days, and by encouragingly large weekday crowds thereafter – 16,594, 17,268 and 12,684, for an aggregate of 93,429. Some unfortunate mistakes by umpires standing in intense heat and uncomfortably aware that every decision would instantly be open to public judgement by replays on the huge electronic scoreboard, marred the conflict. Umpires, unlike scoreboards, have never been machines and never will be. More of this anon. Meanwhile, England undoubtedly, in this match, got the rough end of the stick, and this, plus the loss of the toss, had much to do with their eventual defeat. But it was a defeat which did not hurt for long. The Ashes, after all, were safe and this was a marvellous, fluctuating game, unpredictable to the very end.

Allan Border had now led Australia to three victories at the Sydney Cricket Ground since taking on the captaincy from Kim Hughes and it was his knowledge that the wicket would take increasing spin which persuaded him to bat first, a brave decision, nevertheless, because there was more grass on this than most SCG pitches and, although the grass was dead, it was clear that the seam bowlers would have something to work on.

The two who bowled best for England in the first innings were Phil Edmonds and, again, Gladstone Small, who picked up five wickets and should have had six. He seemed to have Dean Jones brilliantly caught behind off a clean leg-glance when he had made only five, and soon afterwards saw him escape a hard chance to third slip. Thus reprieved, Jones proceeded to play the innings of the match. In Madras a few months previously, his concentration, skill and courage had been rewarded only with a tie. Here he got the eventual reward of playing for the first time in a winning Australian Test team.

Jones's pleasing, upright style, his tight technique and his intensely competitive nature make him certain to be a rock around which Australian batting will be based for a long time. With Border, Marsh and Waugh also firmly established and assuming Ritchie is restored at number five, Australia now need to find a suitable opening partner for Marsh (perhaps Wellham will prove to be the answer, or the forgotten Robbie Kerr or Wayne Phillips) and some consistent bowling support for Reid, who is in a class above the others.

Apart from Jones, who reached 119 not out on the first day and went on to an admirable, handsome, undefeated 184 in nine hours with 12 fours and a six, only Border managed to reach 25 in Australia's first innings. But the tailenders stubbornly occupied the crease, with the redoubtable Taylor to the fore.

Ups and downs for Dean Jones during his match-winning century. This one (top) evaded Richards, though earlier in this innings, when Jones was 5, it was generally thought that Richards had brilliantly caught him. Another close call (above left), but Jones got back just in time against Edmonds. A latter-day Bill Ponsford? Jones (above right) has the look of a man of destiny as he acknowledges what may be the first of many Test hundreds against England.

The fairy-tale unfolds. Peter Taylor during his triumphant and unexpected first Test for Australia. Umpire Steve Randell clearly likes the look of the new boy!

Before this Test match, Taylor, a sandy-haired 30-year-old agricultural scientist, had played in only six first-class matches. A product of Barker's College, one of Sydney's smaller independent schools, he had played for Northern Districts in Sydney Grade cricket for many years as a respected all-rounder and had impressed good judges when touring Zimbabwe with New South Wales in March and April 1986 as well as when playing in the Sheffield Shield final last year when his four for 31 against Queensland prompted Greg Chappell to try to persuade him to move north. Chappell may therefore safely be presumed to have been the mastermind behind the selection of a cricketer who had played only four Sheffield Shield matches and had taken a mere eight first-class wickets in Australia (although he collected 11 wickets in two matches against Zimbabwe). Even Chappell could hardly have dreamt that he would be man of the match in his first Test.

Taylor made his first impact on the second day, starting with a dogged defensive innings in the morning and following this with the wickets of Lamb and Botham in the evening. Lamb, having started impressively, was caught off a bottom edge, cutting, and Botham, after two cuts for four and a huge six over long-on, flicked a big off-break firmly to short-leg where Marsh, Australia's new vice-captain, held an excellent catch. (The selectors had wanted Wellham to be Border's deputy, but had been quickly over-ruled by the ACB, a legacy of Wellham's South African connection.)

It had already been an evening of vivid excitement. First Hughes and Reid only one Woolley, one Sobers and Gower, too, is unique. In one over from Reid he hit four boundaries: a square-cut which became, because he was there too early on the slow pitch, a pull past mid-on; an off-drive; a feathery glance to square-leg; and a regal cover-drive. All this and Taylor too. The crowd went home happy and the Test was the talk of Sydney for the next three days.

Gower became Taylor's third victim early on Monday morning, driving to extra cover, and if Taylor is to prove in time to have any special quality, other than a sound grounding in the game and a very cool temperament, it may be his ability to make the ball dip a little. After Richards,

A crucial moment. David Gower, after a sparkling innings on the Sunday evening, departs after driving Taylor into the safe hands of Dirk Wellham.

broke through with the new ball, claiming Athey, acrobatically caught off his gloves, Gatting narrowly lbw and Broad palpably so, playing no stroke. Then Gower counter-attacked quite gloriously, mellow, thrilling strokes ringing from his bat like echoes of Sobers or Woolley. Yet there was with another confident and impressive innings, and then Emburey, playing with such resources, confidence and skill that at one time a maiden Test hundred seemed possible, had reduced Australia's lead to relatively insignificant proportions, Taylor took the last two wickets with balls which also invited the batsmen to drive.

Australia, building on a lead of 68, made 74 for two by the end of the third day, led by a most assured and confident Border, who quickly got the better of Dilley and then turned more respectful attention to the spinners.

Edmonds got Border out, chopping onto his stumps, early on the fourth day, but it was Emburey, bowling, like his partner, with the handicap of a strained groin, who quickly swept through the middle-order batting on a pitch which, helped by another roasting from an unrelenting sun on the rest day, was now allowing occasionally sharp turn. Nevertheless, Emburey's control, as usual, was superb.

One of the most decisive moments in the whole game occurred shortly before lunch when Waugh, then 15, escaped a straightforward stumping chance to Richards off Edmonds. It was Richards's one really serious blemish in the whole series. From 145 for seven, Waugh led a spirited tail-end revival, the second of the game. The left-handed Taylor, skilfully and intelligently using his pads to defend and his bat to attack, supported him most admirably.

They put on 98 for the eighth wicket, occupying the entire afternoon session. Had their stand been 38 instead, England would have won. But we would also have been denied, quite possibly, the pulsating, nerve-straining finish on the fifth day. No-one should be sorry that the match ended as it did, especially as it proved once more that leg-spinners can still be match-winners. Odd, though, that the original script said that Australia's fast bowlers would win it for them in the first Test at Brisbane, and that England's spinners were bound to be too good for Australia in the last match at Sydney!

The tiredest men of all, undoubtedly, when it was all over, were the two umpires, Steve Randell and Peter McConnell, who were asked to concentrate for six hours a day in intense heat and to make some hairline decisions under pressure from aggressive appealing from both sides and from the unnerving prospect of having their decisions instantly adjudicated by a jury of thousands, many of them ignorant, their evidence being a rapid and often deceptive replay on the electronic scoreboard.

It appears to be hoping for too much for the modern Test player to show more restraint than he does. One sympathizes entirely with the well-known English Test umpire who referred during a recent home series to the two teams being a very pleasant bunch of cricketers. 'Cheats, mind you', he added, 'but nice cheats.'

There were some nice cheats at the Sydney Cricket Ground at the beginning of January. Seldom, outside the Indian sub-continent at any rate, can two umpires have been subjected to so much irresponsible appealing as when Australia were trying, with understandable desperation, to bowl England out on the last day. The umpires, who had not had a very good match, stood up manfully to the unfair pressure. Any mistakes they made were ones of judgement, not, as in the case of one senior Australian umpire in the Perth Challange, the result of ignorance of the laws and very definitely not the result of bias. They deserve better from the players whose duplicity only makes bad decisions more likely, especially in the case of 'bat-pad' catches on turning pitches. On the whole the series was conducted in a friendly spirit by the two teams, even the loquacious Australian wicket-keeper Tim Zoehrer being forgiven (by some) for his excessive exuberance, but Test captains of all countries need to get together before every series to resolve to make appeals only when they really think a batsman might be out.

Perhaps for the only time in the series, the pressure on the umpires got out of hand at Sydney. Tim Zoehrer was the worst offender. He appealed in isolation (top) for a catch off Edmonds's pad. A more worthy shout? But Botham (above left) was not out. Richards (above right) asks for clarification of the wicket-keeper's last debating point.

At least umpires should be spared the instant electronic replay of any but the most clearcut decisions. To see how a batsman got out, or stroked a four, is obviously an advantage for spectators, who can so easily look down at the wrong moment and thus miss a vital incident as it happens. But anything remotely contentious should be left off the public screen. If it is not, there could easily be riots in tense situations in some countries. Indeed it was at Sydney itself – over a century ago – that the first big-match 'riot' occurred as a result, inevitably, of a disputed umpiring decision. This time there was angry booing when Waugh was rightly given out caught, off the glove, in the first innings.

The only alternative is for the umpires themselves, aided by a third umpire with access to every camera angle, to have the benefit of replays before they make their decisions. Even this would not be proof against error, but perhaps it is time for experiments to be carried out in a couple of relatively unimportant one-day internationals.

Moment of victory: Emburey bowled by Sleep with just an over to go. Waugh, Jones, Border and Zoehrer experience the joy of Australia's first win for 14 Tests.

AUSTRALIA v ENGLAND (Fifth Test)

Played at Sydney on 10, 11, 12, 14, 15 January 1987
Toss: Australia. Result: Australia won by 55 runs. Man of the match: P.L. Taylor

AUSTRALIA

G.R. Marsh	c Gatting b Small	24	(2) c Emburey b Dilley	14
G.M. Ritchie	lbw b Dilley	6	(1) c Botham b Edmonds	13
D.M. Jones	not out	184	c Richards b Emburey	30
*A.R. Border	c Botham b Edmonds	34	b Edmonds	49
D.M. Wellham	c Richards b Small	17	c Lamb b Emburey	1
S.R. Waugh	c Richards b Small	0	c Athey b Emburey	73
P.R. Sleep	c Richards b Small	9	c Lamb b Emburey	10
†T.J. Zoehrer	c Gatting b Small	12	lbw b Emburey	1
P.L. Taylor	c Emburey b Edmonds	11	c Lamb b Emburey	42
M.G. Hughes	c Botham b Edmonds	16	b Emburey	5
B.A. Reid	b Dilley	4	not out	1
Extras	(b 12, lb 4, w 2, nb 8)	26	(b 5, lb 7)	12
Total		**343**		**251**

ENGLAND

B.C. Broad	lbw b Hughes	6	c and b Sleep	17
C.W.J. Athey	c Zoehrer b Hughes	5	b Sleep	31
*M.W. Gatting	lbw b Reid	0	(5) c and b Waugh	96
A.J. Lamb	c Zoehrer b Taylor	24	c Waugh b Taylor	3
D.I. Gower	c Wellham b Taylor	72	(3) c Marsh b Border	37
I.T. Botham	c Marsh b Taylor	16	c Wellham b Taylor	0
†C.J. Richards	c Wellham b Reid	46	b Sleep	38
J.E. Emburey	b Taylor	69	b Sleep	22
P.H. Edmonds	c Marsh b Taylor	3	lbw b Sleep	0
G.C. Small	b Taylor	14	c Border b Reid	0
G.R. Dilley	not out	4	not out	2
Extras	(b 9, lb 3, w 2, nb 2)	16	(b 8, lb 6, w 1, nb 3)	18
Total		**275**		**264**

ENGLAND XI	O	M	R	W	O	M	R	W
Dilley	23.5	5	67	2	15	4	48	1
Small	33	11	75	5	8	2	17	0
Botham	23	10	42	0	3	0	17	0
Emburey	30	4	62	0	46	5	78	7
Edmonds	34	5	79	3	43	16	79	2
Gatting	1	0	2	0	2	2	0	0

AUSTRALIA	O	M	R	W	O	M	R	W
Hughes	16	3	58	2	12	3	32	0
Reid	25	7	74	2	19	8	32	1
Waugh	6	4	6	0	6	2	13	1
Taylor	26	7	78	6	29	10	76	2
Sleep	21	6	47	0	35	14	72	5
Border					13	6	25	1

FALL OF WICKETS

	A	E	A	E
Wkt	1st	1st	2nd	2nd
1st	8	16	29	24
2nd	58	17	31	91
3rd	149	17	106	91
4th	184	89	110	102
5th	184	119	115	102
6th	200	142	141	233
7th	232	213	145	257
8th	271	219	243	257
9th	338	270	248	262
10th	343	275	251	264

Umpires: P.J. McConnell and S.G. Randell.

The victor at last. Allan Border receives long-awaited congratulations from his team.

The hill at Sydney, reduced in size now, and carefully
policed but still a good place for the young to see and be seen.

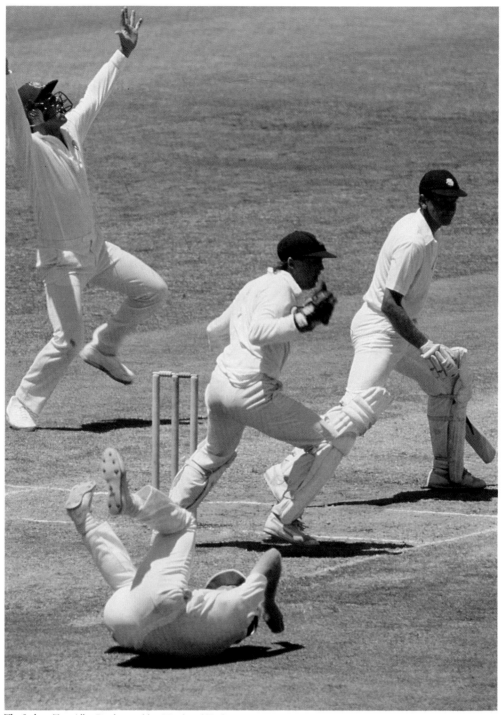

The Sydney Test. Allan Border tumbles, Marsh and Zoehrer
appeal but Bill Athey survives.

Better luck this time! Allan Lamb is out immediately after
lunch on the pulsating last day, caught off bat and pad off
Peter Taylor. Marsh, Zoehrer, Border and the victim react
suitably.

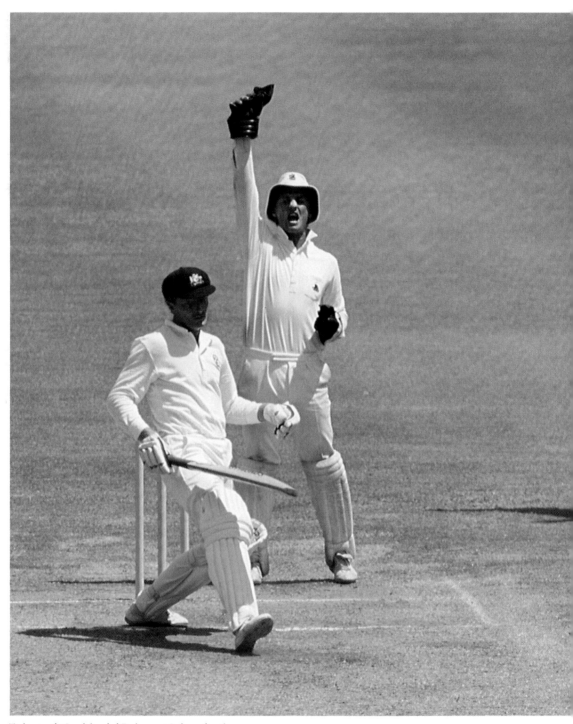

Taylor caught Lamb bowled Emburey at Sydney after the
dogged innings of an experienced Grade cricketer
determined to make the most of his unexpected elevation.

Top: Peter Sleep caught by Lamb off Emburey in the second innings at Sydney.

Above: 'Pom' supporters (presumably!) getting frizzled during England's opening WSC match at Brisbane.

Allan Lamb batting for England in the WSC when he was
frequently the most accomplished of the England batsmen.
But his long run of failures in Test cricket threatens his
future at the highest level.

Like stout Cortez, when with eagle eyes…the skipper in
command, even with a hand in his pocket!

CHAPTER NINE

GRAND SLAM

England arrived in Brisbane nearly an hour late after an early-morning start, very tired after the intense mental and physical pressures of the classically exciting Sydney Test match. With only a few hours to recuperate on this excessively demanding tour they now faced two big matches in hot conditions before big crowds in two days, the first encounters in the Benson and Hedges World Series Cup in which they were to play a minimum of eight matches plus, if they made it, a best of three-game final.

Four weeks later, watched by enthusiastic crowds not only in Australia but also, through live television, by their supporters at home, England completed their clean sweep of the available trophies in the Australian season of 1986–87. It was their first success in this hyped annual triangular tournament of one-day internationals which leave Australians of the old school numbed by their monotonous similarity, year after year.

In 1979–80, the first 'Year of Peace AP' (After Packer), England had reached the final and lost to the West Indies. In 1982–83 they had come a poor third to Australia and New Zealand. This time they earned a telegram from Mrs Thatcher by winning two 'finals' at Melbourne and Sydney, the first comfortably, the second in a tense, low-scoring match in which Simon O'Donnell, after a spirited innings, was not quite equal to the task of emulating Allan Lamb who, in the previous encounter between the two teams at the SCG, had scored 18 runs off the last over to pull the dollars out of the fire.

England's genuine team spirit,

sound and often brilliant catching, admirable professionalism and will to win, carried them through the last weary weeks of an excessively demanding tour. The desperation showed on their faces during the final game at Sydney. The thought of having to play a third 'final' (when is a final a final?) was clearly too awful to contemplate. But with Botham limping, Dilley, Athey and Gower unable to throw, and Broad and Lamb suffering strained hamstrings, they nonetheless scrambled to a victory which earned each man in the 16-man touring team an overall bonus of over £4,000 a head. It may not always be so, but on this tour they earned every penny.

By getting to the finals, Australia found some consolation for their Ashes defeat. Both Jones and Waugh enhanced their growing reputations, and O'Donnell, Davis and Matthews all made a number of telling contributions.

England began the long series of World Series matches with a brave victory in stifling heat at Brisbane over the West Indies, whose sudden vulnerability after years of domination was the real surprise of the tournament. Their batting frailty was the essential reason for their failure to win the World Series Cup for the first time in five attempts. But their bowling was also less effective, partly because neither Garner nor Holding is quite what he was, partly also because Marshall, after a hard tour of Pakistan, was worried by knee and muscle strains. In addition the experimental rule in one-day cricket in Australia, which requires the square-leg umpire to call a no-ball if a short delivery bounces above a batsman's shoulder height, removed much of the venom from bowlers who in recent years

In the WSC, Simon O'Donnell again looked one of Australia's most effective all-round cricketers. Can he translate his form to the Test arena?

have consistently relied on softening batsmen up with short-pitched balls. It is Viv Richards's misfortune that he has taken over as captain at a time when opinion has (belatedly) hardened all round the world against the over-use of the bouncer.

England seemed to be sure of a place in the finals until losing a match on Australia Day in Adelaide against the home team. They were winning this game easily until they paid the penalty for some unintelligent batting, especially against Peter Taylor. They were beaten by West Indies and then by Australia again at Melbourne – Dean Jones to the fore with

93 – so came to the last of their qualifying matches needing to beat the West Indies again at Devonport in Tasmania. With Foster and French now drafted into the side, leaving only poor Wilf Slack totally unemployed in any of the international matches on the tour (five Tests and 14 limited-overs internationals) England rose again to the occasion. Two of their toughest and most experienced players, Botham and Emburey, took three wickets each against a disconsolate West Indies who were without Greenidge and Haynes, the rocks on which many a past victory had been built.

Wait until next time! Greg Matthews symbolizes Australia's current position at the feet of England, but Mike Gatting was wise enough to know that, sooner or later, the wheel will turn.

Here, match by match, are the details of the World Series Cup.

ENGLAND V WEST INDIES
England beat West Indies for the second time in successive one-day internationals. Their success was comfortably achieved thanks to a fine all-round bowling display. Dilley, as he did at Perth, had the best figures and won the man of the match award, and there were composed and confident innings from Broad and Gower.

AUSTRALIA V ENGLAND
England found two consecutive days' cricket in Brisbane's blistering heat, coming straight after their exertions at Sydney, too much and they lost their first one-day international of the tour following five victories. Jones made his fourth hundred of the month from only 101 balls and with the steady support of Marsh added 178 for the second wicket in only 30 overs. England's strokemakers could not quite provide the necessary acceleration so, despite Athey's patient 111, the home side won by 11 runs.

AUSTRALIA V WEST INDIES
A crowd of 63,614 saw West Indies gain their first victory of the competition, joining England and Australia on two points. Border and O'Donnell restored Australia from 74 for five but Haynes partnered by Logie, who was the most consistent of the West Indian batsmen in Australia as well as a brilliant fielder, ensured victory with 10 balls to spare.

ENGLAND v WEST INDIES
Played at Brisbane on 17 January 1987
Toss: England. Result: England won by 6 wickets
Man of the match: G.R. Dilley

WEST INDIES

C.G. Greenidge	lbw b DeFreitas	0
D.L. Haynes	c DeFreitas b Emburey	48
R.B. Richardson	c Botham b Dilley	15
*I.V.A. Richards	b Dilley	0
A.L. Logie	c Lamb b Emburey	46
†P.J.L. Dujon	b DeFreitas	22
R.A. Harper	lbw b Small	2
M.D. Marshall	b Dilley	13
M.A. Holding	c Richards b Emburey	0
J. Garner	c Richards b Dilley	1
C.A. Walsh	not out	3
Extras	(lb 4)	4
Total (46.3 overs)		**154**

ENGLAND

B.C. Broad	b Richards	49
C.W.J. Athey	c Dujon b Holding	14
D.I. Gower	c Garner b Harper	42
A.J. Lamb	c sub (W.K.M. Benjamin) b Harper	22
*M.W.Gatting	not out	3
I.T. Botham	not out	14
†C.J. Richards		
P.A.J. DeFreitas		
J.E. Emburey		
G.C. Small		
G.R. Dilley		
Extras	(lb 2, w 2, nb 8)	12
Total (43.1 overs)	4 wickets	**156**

BOWLING

ENGLAND	O	M	R	W
Dilley	8.3	1	23	4
DeFreitas	9	2	17	2
Botham	10	1	46	0
Small	10	1	29	1
Emburey	9	0	35	3
WEST INDIES				
Marshall	5	1	11	0
Garner	4	0	17	0
Holding	6	0	33	1
Walsh	7.1	0	19	0
Harper	10	0	43	2
Richards	10	1	27	1
Richardson	1	0	4	0

FALL OF WICKETS

	1	2	3	4	5	6	7	8	9	10
WI	1	26	26	112	120	122	147	148	151	154
E	30	91	134	140						

Umpires: M.W. Johnson and P.J. McConnell.

AUSTRALIA v ENGLAND

Played at Brisbane on 18 January 1987
Toss: Australia. Result: Australia won by 11 runs.
Man of the match: D.M. Jones

AUSTRALIA

G.R. Marsh	lbw b Dilley	93
D.M. Wellham	c Emburey b Small	26
D.M. Jones	b Emburey	101
*A.R. Border	b Dilley	11
S.R. Waugh	not out	14
S.P. O'Donnell	not out	3
G.R.J. Matthews		
K.H. Macleay		
†T.J. Zoehrer		
P.L. Taylor		
B.A. Reid		
Extras	(lb 9, w 3, nb 1)	13
Total (50 overs)	4 wickets	**261**

ENGLAND

B.C. Broad	c Matthews b O'Donnell	15
C.W.J. Athey	c O'Donnell b Reid	111
D.I. Gower	b Waugh	15
A.J. Lamb	c Marsh b Matthews	6
I.T. Botham	b O'Donnell	22
*M.W.Gatting	b Taylor	30
†C.J. Richards	c O'Donnell b Reid	7
P.A.J. DeFreitas	c Border b Waugh	6
J.E. Emburey	not out	24
G.C. Small	run out	2
G.R. Dilley	not out	0
Extras	(b 1, lb 10, nb 1)	12
Total (50 overs)	9 wickets	**250**

BOWLING

ENGLAND	O	M	R	W
Dilley	10	2	40	2
DeFreitas	10	2	41	0
Small	10	0	57	1
Botham	10	0	54	0
Emburey	10	0	60	1
AUSTRALIA				
Macleay	8	0	39	0
Reid	10	1	34	2
O'Donnell	10	0	59	2
Waugh	9	0	56	2
Matthews	10	0	34	1
Taylor	3	0	17	1

FALL OF WICKETS

	1	2	3	4	5	6	7	8	9	10
A	48	226	234	246						
E	48	73	92	149	197	210	218	225	250	

Umpires: M.W. Johnson and P.J. McConnell.

AUSTRALIA v WEST INDIES

Played at Melbourne on 20 January 1987
Toss: West Indies. Result: West Indies won by 7 wickets.
Man of the match: D.L. Haynes

AUSTRALIA

G.R. Marsh	Dujon b Garner	1
D.M. Wellham	run out	7
D.M. Jones	lbw b Marshall	11
*A.R. Border	not out	64
S.R. Waugh	hit wkt b Holding	15
G.R.J. Matthews	run out	0
S.P O'Donnell	c Holding b Marshall	52
K.H. Macleay	not out	12
†T.J. Zoehrer		
P.L. Taylor		
B.A. Reid		
Extras	(b 5, lb 4, w 1, nb 9)	19
Total (50 overs)	6 wickets	**181**

WEST INDIES

C.G. Greenidge	c Border b Waugh	35
D.L. Haynes	lbw b Matthews	67
R.B. Richardson	b Taylor	20
A.L. Logie	not out	44
†P.J.L. Dujon	not out	2
*I.V.A. Richards		
R.A. Harper		
M.D. Marshall		
M.A. Holding		
J. Garner		
C.A. Walsh		
Extras	(b 5, lb 3, w 1, nb 3)	14
Total (48.2 overs)	3 wickets	**182**

BOWLING

WEST INDIES	O	M	R	W
Marshall	9	0	40	2
Garner	9	1	47	1
Holding	10	1	15	1
Walsh	10	2	37	0
Harper	10	0	26	0
Richards	2	0	7	0
AUSTRALIA				
Macleay	6	0	20	0
Reid	8.2	2	33	0
O'Donnell	7	0	27	0
Waugh	7	0	30	1
Matthews	10	2	27	1
Taylor	10	1	35	1

FALL OF WICKETS

	1	2	3	4	5	6	7	8	9	10
A	2	23	30	74	74	165				
WI	54	92	171							

Umpires: A.R. Crafter and R.A. French.

AUSTRALIA V ENGLAND

England were behind the clock for virtually the whole of their reply but the expected narrow Australian victory was transformed into an England win by Allan Lamb in extraordinary fashion. With one over left 18 runs were still needed. Lamb was unbeaten on 59 but had not been able to score freely, and he had to face Bruce Reid, the most accurate of the Australian bowlers. He managed two to deep extra-cover off the first ball thanks to a wild throw, he hit the second for four to the unguarded square-leg boundary and the third for a massive six over mid-wicket, he could only guide the third to cover but a poor return and an overthrow allowed him to keep the strike and he was able to hit the winning boundary, again to square-leg, off the fifth. England had nudged ahead in the WSC table in quite remarkable style.

ENGLAND V WEST INDIES

England extended their lead by beating a West Indian team beginning to show signs of running out of steam by a most convincing margin. The Broad–Athey opening partnership once more set them on their way with a stand of 121 in 32 overs, while DeFreitas and Emburey had the best bowling figures, as West Indies lost their first two wickets for 15 and their last six for 27.

AUSTRALIA V WEST INDIES

West Indies again recovered from defeat against England by beating the home country. Richards and Richardson both made their first sizeable contributions of the tournament, and the later Australian batsmen could not build upon the good start provided by Marsh and Jones, Walsh and Harper sharing six wickets.

AUSTRALIA v ENGLAND

Played at Sydney on 22 January 1987
Toss: Australia. Result: England won by 3 wickets
Man of the match: A.J. Lamb

AUSTRALIA

G.R. Marsh	c Richards b Edmonds	47
D.M. Wellham	c Athey b Emburey	97
D.M. Jones	c Athey b DeFreitas	34
*A.R. Border	c Dilley b Edmonds	13
S.R. Waugh	c Athey b Dilley	10
G.R.J. Matthews	c DeFreitas b Emburey	2
K.H. Macleay	b Dilley	12
†T.J. Zoehrer	not out	9
P.L. Taylor	st Richards b Emburey	0
S.P. O'Donnell		
B.A. Reid		
Extras	(b 2, lb 5, nb 2)	9
Total (50 overs)	8 wickets	233

ENGLAND

B.C. Broad	c Matthews b Taylor	45
C.W.J. Athey	c Zoehrer b Reid	2
D.I. Gower	c Wellham b O'Donnell	50
A.J. Lamb	not out	77
*M.W.Gatting	b O'Donnell	1
I.T. Botham	b Waugh	27
J.E. Emburey	run out	4
†C.J. Richards	c Waugh b O'Donnell	3
P.A.J. DeFreitas	not out	6
P.H. Edmonds		
G.R. Dilley		
Extras	(lb 16, w 2, nb 1)	19
Total (49.5 overs)	7 wickets	234

BOWLING

ENGLAND	O	M	R	W
Dilley	9	2	28	2
DeFreitas	10	0	46	1
Gatting	2	0	11	0
Botham	10	0	51	0
Emburey	9	0	42	3
Edmonds	10	0	48	2
AUSTRALIA				
Macleay	4	0	22	0
Reid	9.5	3	44	1
Taylor	10	0	42	1
Waugh	5	0	22	1
Matthews	10	1	36	0
Border	3	0	13	0
O'Donnell	8	0	39	3

FALL OF WICKETS

	1	2	3	4	5	6	7	8	9	10
A	109	156	189	205	208	208	230	233		
E	33	51	137	143	186	191	202			

Umpires: A.R. Crafter and R.A. French.

ENGLAND v WEST INDIES

Played at Adelaide on 24 January 1987
Toss: West Indies. Result: England won by 89 runs.
Man of the match: B.C. Broad

ENGLAND

B.C. Broad	st Dujon b Richards	55
C.W.J. Athey	c Marshall b Harper	64
D.I. Gower	c Haynes b Gray	29
I.T. Botham	c Logie b Walsh	7
A.J. Lamb	not out	33
*M.W. Gatting	c Dujon b Walsh	3
†C.J. Richards	b Marshall	18
J.E. Emburey	not out	16
P.A.J. DeFreitas		
G.C. Small		
G.R. Dilley		
Extras	(b 4, lb 13, w 5, nb 5)	27
Total (50 overs)	6 wickets	252

WEST INDIES

C.G. Greenidge	lbw b DeFreitas	3
D.L. Haynes	b Small	22
R.B. Richardson	c Lamb b DeFreitas	3
*I.V.A. Richards	c Broad b Botham	43
A.L. Logie	c Gower b Dilley	43
†P.J.L. Dujon	c Dilley b Emburey	25
R.A. Harper	c Dilley b Emburey	4
M.D. Marshall	c Athey b Emburey	3
J. Garner	c DeFreitas b Emburey	0
A.H. Gray	not out	7
C.A. Walsh	b DeFreitas	3
Extras	(w 2, nb 5)	7
Total (45.5 overs)		163

BOWLING

WEST INDIES	O	M	R	W
Marshall	9	1	39	1
Gray	10	0	43	1
Garner	9	1	31	0
Walsh	10	0	55	2
Harper	9	0	46	1
Richards	3	0	21	1
ENGLAND				
Dilley	8	1	19	1
DeFreitas	7.5	1	15	3
Botham	10	0	46	1
Small	10	1	46	1
Emburey	10	0	37	4

FALL OF WICKETS

	1	2	3	4	5	6	7	8	9	10
E	121	148	161	177	182	220				
WI	3	15	60	92	136	141	150	150	157	163

Umpires: B.E. Martin and S.G. Randell.

AUSTRALIA v WEST INDIES

Played at Adelaide on 25 January 1987
Toss: Australia. Result: West Indies won by 16 runs.
Man of the match: G.R. Marsh

WEST INDIES

D.L. Haynes	c Zoehrer b Davis	3
R.B. Richardson	b Waugh	72
H.A. Gomes	b Matthews	43
*I.V.A. Richards	c Davis b Waugh	69
A.L. Logie	run out	0
†P.J.L. Dujon	not out	12
R.A. Harper	not out	13
M.D. Marshall		
J. Garner		
A.H. Gray		
C.A. Walsh		
Extras	(b 3, lb 15, w 7)	25
Total (50 overs)	5 wickets	237

AUSTRALIA

G.R. Marsh	c Harper b Walsh	94
D.M. Wellham	c Dujon b Marshall	3
D.M. Jones	lbw b Garner	40
*A.R. Border	b Harper	1
S.R. Waugh	c Richards b Harper	24
G.R.J. Matthews	c and b Harper	3
S.P. O'Donnell	c Dujon b Marshall	0
P.L. Taylor	b Walsh	4
†T.J. Zoehrer	not out	22
B.A. Reid	b Walsh	1
S.P. Davis	not out	3
Extras	(lb 12, w 10, nb 4)	26
Total (50 overs)	9 wickets	221

BOWLING

AUSTRALIA	O	M	R	W
Davis	8	1	21	1
Reid	10	0	43	0
Waugh	7	0	41	2
Matthews	10	0	34	1
O'Donnell	7	0	31	0
Taylor	8	0	49	0
WEST INDIES				
Marshall	10	2	34	2
Gray	10	1	44	0
Garner	10	0	36	1
Walsh	10	0	46	3
Harper	10	0	49	3

FALL OF WICKETS

	1	2	3	4	5	6	7	8	9	10
WI	18	110	184	184	221					
A	4	85	86	158	171	172	183	199	217	

Umpires: R.A. Bailache and A.R. Crafter.

AUSTRALIA V ENGLAND

At 125 for two, needing 101 in 19 overs, England looked on course to sew up their place in the finals with three matches to spare but Taylor's gentle off-spin produced a series of reckless shots and they lost their last seven wickets for 67 to fall 33 runs short. Border and Waugh, who later picked up two wickets, shared a fourth-wicket partnership of 164 from a perilous position of 37 for three.

AUSTRALIA V WEST INDIES

It was Australia's turn to beat West Indies as their bowlers were unable to defend successfully a relatively modest total. O'Donnell, who won the man of the match award, Waugh and Matthews showed once more what useful one-day performers they are. Even Richards could not break out of the shackles they imposed.

ENGLAND V WEST INDIES

England could not recover from a shaky start, slipping to 37 for three, 77 for five and 111 for seven but, although West Indies were never in danger of losing, their batsmen could not score fast enough on an awkward pitch against more impressive English bowling to improve their disappointing run-rate. Richards, with two sixes from successive balls off Emburey, became the first batsman to make 5,000 runs in one-day internationals.

AUSTRALIA v ENGLAND

Played at Adelaide on 26 January 1987
Toss: Australia. Result: Australia won by 33 runs.
Man of the match: S.R. Waugh

AUSTRALIA

G.R. Marsh	c Emburey b DeFreitas	8
D.M. Wellham	c Richards b DeFreitas	9
D.M. Jones	c Richards b DeFreitas	8
*A.R. Border	c Broad b DeFreitas	91
S.R. Waugh	not out	83
S.P. O'Donnell	run out	6
G.R.J. Matthews	c Lamb b Dilley	0
†T.J. Zoehrer	not out	5
K.H. Macleay		
P.L. Taylor		
S.P. Davis		
Extras	(b 1, lb 8, w 4, nb 2)	15
Total (50 overs)	6 wickets	225

ENGLAND

B.C. Broad	c Border b Waugh	46
C.W.J. Athey	lbw b Davis	12
D.I. Gower	c Waugh b O'Donnell	21
*M.W. Gatting	b Taylor	46
A.J. Lamb	run out	8
I.T. Botham	st Zoehrer b Taylor	18
†C.J. Richards	b Waugh	2
J.E. Emburey	run out	17
P.A.J. DeFreitas	c Jones b Taylor	8
G.C. Small	b Macleay	2
G.R. Dilley	not out	3
Extras	(lb 8, w 1)	9
Total (48.1 overs)		192

BOWLING

ENGLAND	O	M	R	W
Dilley	10	1	41	1
DeFreitas	10	1	35	4
Botham	10	0	42	0
Small	10	0	42	0
Emburey	10	0	56	0
AUSTRALIA				
Davis	8	0	18	1
Macleay	10	1	43	1
Matthews	4	0	21	0
O'Donnell	9	0	43	1
Waugh	10	1	30	2
Taylor	7.1	0	29	3

FALL OF WICKETS

	1	2	3	4	5	6	7	8	9	10
A	21	24	37	201	211	219				
E	23	55	125	138	144	152	168	184	188	192

Umpires: A.R Crafter and S.G. Randell.

AUSTRALIA v WEST INDIES

Played at Sydney on 28 January 1987
Toss: Australia. Result: Australia won by 36 runs
Man of the match: S.P. O'Donnell

AUSTRALIA

G.R. Marsh	c Garner b Walsh	20
*A.R. Border	hit wkt b Walsh	19
D.M. Jones	c Richards b Benjamin	22
G.M. Ritchie	c Haynes b Garner	35
D.M. Wellham	c Dujon b Marshall	39
S.R. Waugh	run out	16
S.P O'Donnell	run out	6
†T.J. Zoehrer	run out	1
G.R.J. Matthews	not out	13
P.L. Taylor	c Dujon b Marshall	2
S.P. Davis	run out	3
Extras	(b 3, lb 10, w 3, nb 2)	18
Total (50 overs)		**194**

WEST INDIES

D.L. Haynes	b Matthews	17
R.B. Richardson	c Zoehrer b O'Donnell	0
H.A. Gomes	c and b O'Donnell	1
*I.V.A. Richards	c Zoehrer b Matthews	70
A.L. Logie	c Wellham b Waugh	2
†P.J.L. Dujon	c Wellham b Waugh	14
R.A. Harper	not out	20
M.D. Marshall	c Waugh b O'Donnell	2
W.K.M. Benjamin	c Zoehrer b O'Donnell	5
J. Garner	c and b Taylor	18
C.A. Walsh	c Border b Matthews	3
Extras	(b 2, lb 2, w 2)	6
Total (46.1 overs)		**158**

BOWLING

WEST INDIES	O	M	R	W
Marshall	10	1	29	2
Garner	10	1	32	1
Walsh	10	1	41	2
Benjamin	10	0	45	1
Harper	10	0	34	0
AUSTRALIA				
Davis	8	0	29	0
O'Donnell	10	2	19	4
Waugh	10	1	21	2
Matthews	8.1	2	32	3
Taylor	10	1	53	1

FALL OF WICKETS

	1	2	3	4	5	6	7	8	9	10
A	33	58	69	112	158	170	173	179	187	194
WI	12	14	40	59	89	114	126	133	152	158

Umpires: R.A. French and M.W. Johnson.

ENGLAND v WEST INDIES

Played at Melbourne on 30 January 1987
Toss: England. Result: West Indies won by 6 wickets
Man of the match: I.V.A. Richards

ENGLAND

B.C. Broad	c Garner b Holding	33
C.W.J. Athey	lbw b Garner	2
D.I. Gower	b Marshall	8
A.J. Lamb	run out	0
*M.W. Gatting	b Harper	13
I.T. Botham	c and b Holding	15
J.E. Emburey	c Harper b Garner	34
†C.J. Richards	b Marshall	8
P.A.J. DeFreitas	c Haynes b Garner	13
N.A. Foster	b Marshall	5
G.C. Small	not out	1
Extras	(lb 3, w 4, nb 8)	15
Total (48.2 overs)		**147**

WEST INDIES

D.L. Haynes	lbw Foster	13
R.B. Richardson	c Richards b DeFreitas	0
H.A. Gomes	run out	36
*I.V.A. Richards	b Foster	58
A.L. Logie	not out	19
†P.J.L. Dujon	not out	1
R.A. Harper		
M.D. Marshall		
M.A. Holding		
J. Garner		
C.A. Walsh		
Extras	(lb 10, w 8, nb 3)	21
Total (48.3 overs)	4 wickets	**148**

BOWLING

WEST INDIES	O	M	R	W
Marshall	9.2	2	30	3
Garner	9	1	37	3
Holding	8.3	2	19	2
Walsh	5	1	16	0
Harper	10	0	26	1
Richards	6.3	1	16	0
ENGLAND				
DeFreitas	10	2	15	1
Small	10	3	16	0
Botham	10	3	28	0
Foster	9	1	25	2
Emburey	9.3	1	54	0

FALL OF WICKETS

	1	2	3	4	5	6	7	8	9	10
E	11	27	37	61	77	84	111	136	144	147
WI	7	49	98	146						

Umpires: R.C. Bailhache and S.G. Randell.

AUSTRALIA V ENGLAND

Australia became the first side to qualify for the finals with an emphatic victory but English minds began to think of an early return home as they suffered their third successive defeat. Jones and Waugh were chiefly responsible for the home success in front of a crowd of 58,580.

ENGLAND V WEST INDIES

With their fourth victory over West Indies in five attempts this winter, England joined Australia (barring miracles in the final qualifying game) in the WSC finals. Broad, despite a serious hamstring injury, held the England innings together for 46 overs, and only Lamb and DeFreitas of the other batsmen reached double figures. Even without Dilley, suffering from a shoulder strain, the bowlers successfully contained a weakened West Indian line-up. Botham picked up three important wickets as they slipped from 71 for two to 95 for six, then Emburey finished the match with three wickets in an over.

AUSTRALIA V WEST INDIES

West Indies' attempt to make 374 in their 50 overs and so still qualify for the finals on superior run-rate was unsuccessful and England's final place confirmed. The West Indians' disappointing tour of Australia ended with another defeat, their seventh in 11 one-day internationals, despite 60 from stand-in opener Thelston Payne. Zoehrer, promoted to open for Australia, reached a sparkling fifty in 59 balls.

Final Qualifying Table

	P	W	L	Pts	Rate
Australia	8	5	3	10	4.40
England	8	4	4	8	3.93
West Indies	8	3	5	6	3.48

Player of the WSC preliminary rounds:
I.V.A. Richards

AUSTRALIA v ENGLAND

Played at Melbourne on 1 February 1987
Toss: England. Result: Australia won by 109 runs.
Man of the match: S.R. Waugh

AUSTRALIA
G.R. Marsh	c Emburey b Foster	28
*A.R. Border	c Athey b Small	45
D.M. Jones	c Athey b Gatting	93
G.M. Ritchie	st French b Gatting	9
D.M. Wellham	c Lamb b Gatting	3
S.R. Waugh	not out	49
S.P. O'Donnell	not out	4
†T.J. Zoehrer		
G.R.J. Matthews		
P.L. Taylor		
S.P. Davis		
Extras	(lb 7, w 9, nb 1)	17
Total (50 overs)	5 wickets	248

ENGLAND
B.C. Broad	b O'Donnell	2
I.T. Botham	c and b Matthews	45
D.I. Gower	c Taylor b Davis	11
A.J. Lamb	run out	11
*M.W. Gatting	c Davis b Waugh	6
C.W.J. Athey	lbw b O'Donnell	29
J.E. Emburey	b Matthews	1
P.A.J. DeFreitas	b Waugh	11
N.A. Foster	b Waugh	4
†B.N. French	not out	5
G.C. Small	c Matthews b Jones	4
Extras	(b 2, lb 7, w 1)	10
Total (47.3 overs)		139

BOWLING
ENGLAND	O	M	R	W
DeFreitas	8	2	37	0
Small	10	0	49	1
Botham	10	0	35	0
Foster	7	1	20	1
Emburey	6	0	41	0
Gatting	9	0	59	3
AUSTRALIA				
Davis	8	1	20	1
O'Donnell	9	2	33	2
Matthews	10	1	24	2
Waugh	10	0	26	3
Taylor	9	1	23	0
Jones	1.3	0	4	1

FALL OF WICKETS
	1	2	3	4	5	6	7	8	9	10
A	61	127	144	154	223					
E	4	25	52	65	86	90	117	129	130	139

Umpires: R.A. French and B.E. Martin.

ENGLAND v WEST INDIES

Played at Devonport on 3 February 1987
Toss: West Indies. Result: England won by 29 runs.
Man of the match: B.C. Broad

ENGLAND

B.C. Broad	c Dujon b Walsh	76
I.T.Botham	c Richardson b Gray	8
D.I. Gower	c Payne b Marshall	3
A.J. Lamb	c Logie b Harper	36
*M.W. Gatting	c Richardson b Gray	6
C.W.J. Athey	lbw b Marshall	3
J.E. Emburey	c Garner b Walsh	2
P.A.J. DeFreitas	not out	15
N.A. Foster	run out	0
†B.N. French	b Marshall	0
G.C. Small	not out	6
Extras	(lb 14, w 3, nb 5)	22
Total (50 overs)	9 wickets	177

WEST INDIES

R.B. Richardson	c French b DeFreitas	2
T.R.O. Payne	c French b Botham	18
A.L. Logie	b Foster	31
H.A. Gomes	c Emburey b Botham	19
*I.V.A. Richards	b Botham	1
†P.J.L. Dujon	c Gatting b Emburey	34
R.A. Harper	c French b Small	4
M.D. Marshall	c Athey b DeFreitas	27
J. Garner	b Emburey	4
A.H. Gray	c and b Emburey	0
C.A. Walsh	not out	1
Extras	(lb 5, w 2)	7
Total (48 overs)		148

BOWLING

WEST INDIES	O	M	R	W
Marshall	10	0	31	3
Gray	10	2	29	2
Garner	10	0	30	0
Walsh	10	1	31	2
Harper	10	0	42	1
ENGLAND				
DeFreitas	9	1	20	2
Small	10	0	35	1
Foster	10	0	29	1
Botham	10	1	33	3
Emburey	9	0	26	3

FALL OF WICKETS

	1	2	3	4	5	6	7	8	9	10
E	23	29	103	129	133	143	158	159	160	
WI	10	25	71	73	90	95	132	147	147	148

Umpires: A.R. Crafter and S.G. Randell.

AUSTRALIA v WEST INDIES

Played at Sydney on 6 February 1987
Toss: West Indies. Result: Australia won by 2 wickets.
Man of the match: T.J. Zoehrer

WEST INDIES

R.B. Richardson	c Ritchie b Davis	11
T.R.O. Payne	c and b Taylor	60
A.L. Logie	c Zoehrer b Waugh	14
*I.V.A. Richards	c and b Matthews	25
H.A. Gomes	run out	38
†P.J.L. Dujon	lbw b Taylor	2
R.A. Harper	c Wellham b Davis	20
W.K.M. Benjamin	c Wellham b Taylor	8
J. Garner	run out	6
A.H. Gray	run out	1
C.A. Walsh	not out	1
Extras	(b 1, lb 3, w 2)	6
Total (49 overs)		192

AUSTRALIA

G.R. Marsh	c Richardson b Harper	33
†T.J. Zoehrer	c Richards b Walsh	50
D.M. Jones	c and b Harper	7
G.M. Ritchie	c and b Garner	25
D.M. Wellham	c Garner b Gray	24
S.R. Waugh	st Dujon b Richards	11
*A.R. Border	b Richards	8
S.P. O'Donnell	not out	23
G.R.J. Matthews	b Richards	0
P.L. Taylor	not out	0
S.P. Davis		
Extras	(b 8, lb 3, w 2, nb 1)	14
Total (49.1 overs)	8 wickets	195

BOWLING

AUSTRALIA	O	M	R	W
Davis	10	3	31	2
O'Donnell	10	1	33	0
Waugh	9	1	41	1
Matthews	10	0	47	1
Taylor	10	0	36	3
WEST INDIES				
Garner	10	1	37	1
Gray	8	0	48	1
Benjamin	3.1	1	15	0
Walsh	10	2	16	1
Harper	10	1	34	2
Richards	7	0	29	3
Gomes	1	0	5	0

FALL OF WICKETS

	1	2	3	4	5	6	7	8	9	10
WI	20	35	70	148	152	174	177	187	190	192
A	74	87	106	131	155	163	191	191		

Umpires: R.A. French and P.J. McConnell.

AUSTRALIA V ENGLAND (1st FINAL)
England won the first match of the best-of-three final series with eight overs to spare thanks to another sound bowling performance in helpful conditions and a remarkable 71 in 52 balls from Ian Botham. Early-morning rain delayed the start and Dilley and DeFreitas both took a wicket in their opening overs to rock Australia back at three for two. Then the later home batsmen could not capitalize on a century third-wicket stand by Jones and Border. Botham quickly put the result beyond any doubt by reaching his fifty from 36 balls as he launched a vicious attack on the Australian seam bowlers. In all he hit 11 fours and a towering straight six, dominating an opening stand of 91, before he lofted Matthews's first ball (the first of the 15th over) to mid-off. Some beautifully timed strokes from Gower ensured a comfortable victory.

AUSTRALIA V ENGLAND (2nd FINAL)
England completed a grand slam of tournament victories, a well-deserved reward for their winter's hard work, by restricting Australia to 179 for eight as they chased 188 to win under the Sydney lights. Broad celebrated being named the player of the season by passing 1,000 runs in international cricket on the tour, as he made his fifth one-day fifty to add to three Test hundreds. But it was another highly professional bowling performance and some razor-sharp fielding which sealed their 10th win in 14 one-day internationals. Dilley and DeFreitas, who was the competition's leading wicket-taker, both bowled excellent opening spells. Emburey was naggingly accurate and Botham bade farewell to international cricket overseas with three wickets and the man of the finals award. O'Donnell's best efforts were in vain.

Broader still and Broader! Chris Broad during his 53 in the second final at Sydney when he passed 1,000 runs in all matches on the tour.

AUSTRALIA v ENGLAND (1st Final)

Played at Melbourne on 8 February 1987
Toss: England. Result: England won by 6 wickets.

AUSTRALIA

G.R. Marsh	c Gatting b DeFreitas	2
†T.J. Zoehrer	c Gatting b Dilley	0
D.M. Jones	b DeFreitas	67
*A.R. Border	c French b Foster	42
G.M. Ritchie	run out	13
S.R. Waugh	c DeFreitas b Emburey	1
S.P. O'Donnell	b Dilley	10
G.R.J. Matthews	b Dilley	8
P.L. Taylor	not out	3
B.A. Reid	not out	5
S.P. Davis		
Extras	(lb 10, w 3, nb 7)	20
Total (44 overs)	8 wickets	171

ENGLAND

B.C. Broad	c Jones b Matthews	12
I.T. Botham	c Marsh b Matthews	71
C.W.J. Athey	c and b Matthews	12
D.I. Gower	c Taylor b Reid	45
A.J. Lamb	not out	15
*M.W. Gatting	not out	3
J.E. Emburey		
P.A.J. DeFreitas		
N.A. Foster		
†B.N. French		
G.R. Dilley		
Extras	(b 5, lb 3, w 4, nb 2))	14
Total (36 overs)	4 wickets	172

BOWLING

ENGLAND	O	M	R	W
Dilley	9	2	32	3
DeFreitas	9	0	32	2
Botham	9	0	26	0
Foster	9	0	42	1
Emburey	8	0	29	1
AUSTRALIA				
Davis	4	0	17	0
O'Donnell	4	0	25	0
Reid	5	0	31	1
Waugh	8	1	36	0
Matthews	9	1	27	3
Taylor	5	0	24	0
Jones	1	0	4	0

FALL OF WICKETS

	1	2	3	4	5	6	7	8	9	10
A	3	3	106	134	137	146	161	164		
E	91	93	147	159						

Umpires: P.J. McConnell and S.G. Randell.

AUSTRALIA v ENGLAND (2nd Final)

Played at Sydney on 11 February 1987
Toss: England. Result: England won by 8 runs.
Man of the finals: I.T. Botham

ENGLAND

B.C. Broad	c O'Donnell b Matthews	53
I.T. Botham	c Ritchie b O'Donnell	25
C.W.J. Athey	b Matthews	16
D.I. Gower	c Wellham b Taylor	17
* M.W. Gatting	run out	7
A.J. Lamb	c Zoehrer b O'Donnell	35
J.E. Emburey	c Zoehrer b Waugh	6
P.A.J. DeFreitas	c Jones b Taylor	1
N.A. Foster	c Taylor b Davis	7
†B.N. French	not out	9
G.R. Dilley	not out	6
Extras	(lb 4, w 1)	5
Total (50 overs)	9 wickets	187

AUSTRALIA

G.R. Marsh	lbw b Botham	28
*A.R. Border	c French b Botham	27
D.M. Jones	c and b Emburey	13
G.M. Ritchie	c DeFreitas b Botham	4
D.M. Wellham	c Gower b DeFreitas	30
S.R Waugh	run out	22
S.P. O'Donnell	not out	40
†T.J. Zoehrer	lbw b DeFreitas	0
G.R.J. Matthews	run out	3
P.L. Taylor	not out	3
S.P. Davis		
Extras	(b 1, lb 6, w 2)	9
Total (50 overs)	8 wickets	179

BOWLING

AUSTRALIA	O	M	R	W
Davis	10	0	44	1
O'Donnell	10	1	37	2
Waugh	10	0	42	1
Matthews	10	1	31	2
Taylor	10	2	29	2
ENGLAND				
Dilley	10	1	34	0
DeFreitas	10	1	34	2
Botham	10	1	26	3
Foster	10	0	51	0
Emburey	10	2	27	1

FALL OF WICKETS

	1	2	3	4	5	6	7	8	9	10
E	36	73	102	120	121	143	146	170	170	
A	55	70	72	80	124	135	135	151		

Umpires: A.R. Crafter and R.A. French.

It was a team effort. Bruce French has good reason to smile again, having regained his place at the end of the tour. With him in the final at Sydney are Athey, DeFreitas, Broad and Small, who was fielding as substitute for the injured Botham.

CHAPTER TEN

VERDICT ON A BREATHLESS TOUR

It was over at last. Before returning to a heroes' welcome in London, England's happy, weary players, let their hair down at a party in their apartments near Bondi Beach in Sydney which attracted the only nasty news story of the tour. This in itself was an achievement almost equal to the retention of the Ashes, for the most depressing feature of the previous tour, of the West Indies, had been the frequency of the front-page reports, most but by no means all of them unfair or inaccurate, about behaviour unbecoming to a team of professional cricketers representing their country overseas.

It was not the least of the many happy aspects of the Australian trip that Ian Botham, the chief target of the popular Press, behaved himself impeccably off the field in addition to contributing unselfishly and in full measure on it. Nor did any of his colleagues let themselves down by putting 'birds and booze' before the main objectives of the tour: to keep the Ashes and win as many other games as possible. Much credit for this must go to the managers and captain, though the latter, ironically, was the only man to be officially reprimanded, having overslept after a late night and failed to appear at the start of the Sir Robert Menzies Memorial Match against Victoria.

Gatting is a merry character, full of joie de vivre, who enjoys himself off the field as everyone has a right to do. But he has never been known before to let a late night interfere with his cricket and, characteristically, he was quickly making amends by taking valuable wickets against Victoria. He knew only too well that he had badly let down both himself and his team, though accumulated jet-lag gave him some excuse. As the Sunday newspapers got tucked into the first hint of a 'story' on the tour, I took a private bet that Gatting would react with a century in the Adelaide Test. He obligingly won me a few dollars.

Mike Gatting is genuinely of the bulldog breed and he was so popular and respected both by his team and the travelling Press of both countries that the incident quickly became a joking matter. 'Would everyone please talk quietly,' crooned an Ansett air-hostess as we took off on the flight from Melbourne to Adelaide, 'so that Mr Gatting can catch up on some sleep.'

Gatting's reputation, high enough amongst good judges before he left, was greatly enhanced in the minds of the wider public by the time that he returned, only the third England captain since the war to retain the Ashes in Australia. He should have batted at number three in the one-day matches as well as in the Tests in my view, because his assertiveness makes him so valuable there in any kind of cricket, but generally both his strategy and his tactics were sound throughout the tour. His decision to take over from Gower at three in Brisbane was a decisive moment. At Adelaide and Sydney his batting fairly bristled with character and authority.

Gatting certainly owed much to the support he got from the managers, Peter Lush and Mickey Stewart. Only in the 'affair of the sleeping captain' did Mr Lush get things wrong, letting the matter fester for two or three days instead of telling the true story straightaway and taking any necessary disciplinary action much more quickly than he did. But as administrator and as bridge between the team and the all-pervasive media he was efficient, coolly reliable and sensible.

Mickey Stewart, the 'right man in the right place at the right time'.

John Emburey proved a sound choice as Gatting's deputy, though he would no doubt have made the same positive contribution in all respects even if he had been merely a senior professional, with David Gower the official vice-captain, instead of starting the tour, as he did, as one of the ranks, an unnecessary insult to the most experienced Test cricketer in the party and to the man who had led England to victory in the previous Ashes series less than two years before. But this, of course, was not Emburey's fault. He bowled beautifully at the beginning and end of the tour and the Australians may not even have realized the fact that he had lost some confidence and control in the middle of the tour, disrupted as his rhythm was for a while by the constant breezes which blow across the arid continent. His batting was effective time and again at moments when it needed to be and he took some of the most brilliant of the many good catches held by members of the touring team. Not least, his tactical brain was a useful prop to Gatting, just as it is when they scheme together for Middlesex. Moreover he worked well in harness with Phil Edmonds, who had a most effective tour, playing a full part in the Tests although, in my view, he was under-used in the one-day internationals.

Ian Botham's performances, interrupted as they were by his muscle injury, went in fits and starts, yet he has seldom, if ever, made such an important contribution to a tour. The captain and management were fortunate that the great all-rounder was determined to enjoy a successful last tour. His influence this time was entirely for the good of those around him. He was helpful to the younger players, not least Phillip DeFreitas; sporting, as usual, to his opponents, whom he humours with a sort of superior bonhomie rather as Fred Trueman used to; and he made telling contributions to the Test victories at Brisbane and Melbourne as well as to the many limited-overs successes.

I have mentioned the unwise slight to David Gower's self-esteem. For a time it undoubtedly affected him but he fought back admirably from his early slough of despond and disillusionment and charmed Australian crowds with the grace and poetry of his batting. Of few other players is there such pleasurable anticipation when he walks out and many an Australian finds himself thinking: 'I hope England do badly but that Gower does well.'

Middlesex at the helm. John Emburey was a positive support to Mike Gatting in every way, although he would no doubt have been so whether or not he had been vice-captain.

Chris Broad, of course, stood out above all the batsmen. Except in his 'modern' stance with the bat raised prematurely, he adheres assiduously to the first principles of batting. He is brave, cool, profoundly determined and, which was so important on this tour, as it is in county cricket, has an unusual ability to switch from a 'first-class' mode to a limited-overs one. It is easier to do so, obviously, if you are an opening batsman.

Broad's opening partner, Bill Athey, was equally single-minded and almost equally important to the success of the whole campaign. He fielded like a terrier and batted with neatness and determination. It will be very interesting to see how much more Test cricket he plays and how much further he can raise his present disappointing Test average. He probably needs only to make one Test hundred to get into a habit of making them. He is nowhere near as good as Ken Barrington, yet he has some of the same qualities.

Allan Lamb made his usual positive contribution to the morale of the team throughout. He would find something to smile about in a nuclear winter. But there was a marked difference between his failures in the Tests – which have now gone on for too long to be overlooked – and his often dazzling contributions in the one-day games. If Botham had hit 18 off five balls when 18 were needed off six, people would have said: 'Only Botham could have done that!'

The Gatting/Botham relationship worked. Not necessarily the greatest of friends, they nevertheless respected each other's ability and it was Gatting's good fortune that 'the gorilla' was so anxious to make a success of his final tour for England.

James Whitaker and Wilf Slack were the unlucky batsmen. Whitaker scored more than half his total of runs in one of the seven innings he was allowed to play, excluding country games. Seven innings in four months: what an itinerary! Slack was allowed nine knocks in the same number of games – five. He did not do himself justice; nor, once, did he whinge.

For most of the tour one felt even sorrier for Bruce French than for Slack, Whitaker, and the other long-time passenger, Neil Foster. After a series of rotten misfortunes – losing his place unjustly, losing a best friend, and falling ill – French, happily, won his place back for the last batch of one-day games. Time will tell if it was just a temporary reprieve

because Jack Richards, after an uncertain start, batted outstandingly at Perth and very well at both Adelaide and Sydney. Generally, he kept effectively as well as spectacularly, which is not always the same thing.

The fast bowling stars, in order, of their significance, were Graham Dilley, Gladstone Small and Phillip DeFreitas. Dilley at last took five wickets in a Test innings and bowled with much more confidence than ever he has before, swinging the Kookaburra balls more consistently than he does the English ones. Small was a model of consistency and determination, reliable in all conditions. He may well finish with more Test wickets for England than Dilley himself.

James Whitaker (left) scored more than half his runs in one innings but his opportunities were all too few. Wilf Slack (right) had two more chances at the wicket but spent most of his time in the nets. He kept on smiling!

Graham Dilley had matured, as both a man and a bowler. The tour marked a watershed in his career, not least because of his decision to leave Kent.

Gladstone Small's success was well-deserved. No one bowled more consistently and none was more popular in the dressing-room.

DeFreitas was a willing learner and a rapid one. It was not just youthful zest which enabled him to bowl better than anyone towards the end of the tour. He has mental stamina as well as physical. He is quick enough, and will get quicker; his batting is loose, but unselfish and full of potential; and his fielding in the deep was brilliant (so, indeed, was Small's).

Neil Foster did not make the 'first' team until the very end yet he took his disappointments like a man and managed to enhance his reputation by picking up 16 first-class wickets at an average of 22 in the four matches he played and making 172 runs at 43 in six innings. He is still improving and not to be ruled out of England's future plans.

Phillip DeFreitas proved a wise selection, his immense natural ability, inner drive and youthful zest enabling him to reach his peak late in the tour when others were fading. If he keeps his feet on the ground he has a golden future.

What, finally, of Australia's future? It may not be so bleak as at times it looked. There is a strong batting side, lacking, as mentioned earlier, only a settled opening partner for the admirably correct and determined Geoff Marsh. I am not convinced, however, that Zoehrer is the answer as the wicket-keeper, and the fast-bowling cupboard seemed bare apart from Bruce Reid. Craig McDermott, however, will surely live again for Australia if can apply some brain to make the most of his formidable brawn. Peter Taylor was the happiest of discoveries and it will be fascinating to see how he progresses after his startling late arrival on the stage.

Two things have contributed to Australia's current malaise, and neither is without a parallel in the United Kingdom. The first is the impoverishment of Australia's reserve strength by the enticement of several of the nation's best players to go to South Africa. Cricketers like Kim Hughes and Terry Alderman are not replaced overnight and even if there are not many players currently engaged in South Africa who would neccessarily be involved in the Ashes series, nevertheless their absence reduces the pool of available players and weakens the competition in the Sheffield Shield, the training-ground for Test cricketers.

The other reason goes back further than the South African intrusions. Australia indulges in far too much cricket of a flippant, insignificant and forgettable nature. I refer of course to the absurd excess of limited-overs internationals which every season here since 1979, when World Series Cricket reached an uneasy truce with the Australian Cricket Board, has received star billing from Mr Packer's former company, PBL Marketing, who promote the game ostensibly in the interests of 'cricket' but primarily in the interests of no-one but themselves.

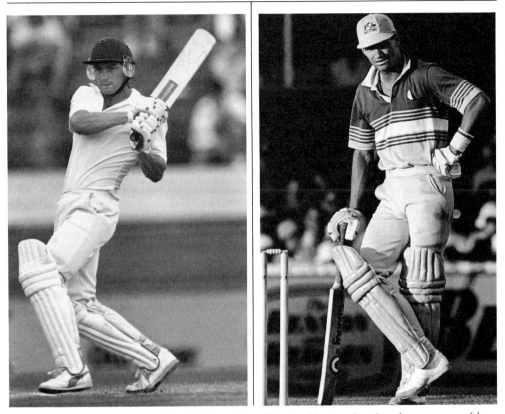

Dean Jones (left), who along with Geoff Marsh (right) and Steve Waugh enables Australia to hope for a more successful future.

Channel Nine and PBL, both now owned by the Perth multi-millionaire, Alan Bond, will continue to televise and market cricket until 1989, when their contracts with the Australian Cricket Board run out. There may be some changes thereafter, but most of those would probably have occurred anyway.

The number of one-day internationals to be played each season was specified in the ten-year agreement made between the ACB and Kerry Packer in 1979. So in the next two seasons Bond is destined to oversee a heavy programme of one-day cricket, and there is no reason to suppose that his income from TV advertising and PBL's share of the gate receipts will be any less than Packer's in recent years. Indeed, having added Packer's Channel Nine stations in Sydney and Melbourne – the most lucrative TV operations in Australia – to his old stations in Perth and Brisbane, Bond could now reach just on 60 per cent of the population of Australia.

Unlike Packer, however, Bond will have no personal axe to grind with the ACB. It seems probable that there will be a modest reduction in one-day internationals after 1989, probably from the recent average of 18 to 12.

Although the 1986–87 England tour confirmed the trend for Australian spectators to prefer the limited-overs games to the Tests, the ACB will be more strongly placed in 1989 to drive a hard

Bruce Reid was Australia's only really consistent bowler. He looks too frail to hold an attack together but if he can find an inswinger he could become a prolific wicket-taker in Tests.

bargain with Bond than they were in 1979 with Packer. If the ACB can ensure that it retains more of the income from the game in future, it should be able to afford to reduce the number of one-day internationals and still put plenty of money back into the grass roots. If there were six fewer WSC matches each year, and no special competitions such as the Perth Challenge, the international programme would be cut by ten days or two weeks. That would allow the Australian players to play a couple of Shield games during January, and the visiting players to play State games, something that would benefit the reserve players in the touring parties, who in recent years have had such a rotten time. If one WSC game were to be cut at each of the five Test grounds, and the only game in Tasmania (unfortunately) cut as well, there is a good chance that the remaining games in Sydney and Melbourne (which have the two largest grounds) would be even better attended.

The ACB will need moral and practical support from administrators from the other Test countries. I have suggested before that world administrators should abandon their obsession with money-making and agree to a self-denying ordinance by which each country would agree to a maximum number of Tests and one-day internationals in any year. Australia, by far the worst culprits, need to diet themselves more than anyone.

Indeed it is precisely the fact that so many Tests are played that Australia's team now appears to be worse than it actually is. England's success came, after all, only a few months after their defeat at home by India and New Zealand and it was only a few months further back to the horrors of the Caribbean. If they were to leave for the West Indies now, the England team, in their Australian mood and form, with Mike Gatting as captain and the

increasingly influential Mickey Stewart cracking the whip when necessary as cricket manager, might draw a Test match or two against what remains the best side in the world. They would almost certainly have little trouble in reversing last season's results against the other two countries. Never has there been a better example than on this tour of the old dictum that 'success breeds success'.

TOUR STATISTICS

AUSTRALIA v ENGLAND 1986–87 TEST AVERAGES

ENGLAND BATTING AND FIELDING

	M	I	NO	R	HS	A	100	50	ct	st
B.C. Broad	5	9	2	487	162	69.57	3	—	5	—
D.I. Gower	5	8	1	404	136	57.71	1	2	1	—
M.W. Gatting	5	9	0	393	100	43.66	1	3	5	—
C.J. Richards	5	7	0	264	133	37.71	1	—	15	1
J.E. Emburey	5	7	2	179	69	35.80	—	1	3	—
C.W.J. Athey	5	9	0	303	96	33.66	—	3	3	—
I.T. Botham	4	6	0	189	138	31.50	1	—	10	—
P.A.J. DeFreitas	4	5	1	77	40	19.25	—	—	1	—
A.J. Lamb	5	9	1	144	43	18.00	—	—	6	—
G.C. Small	2	3	1	35	21*	17.50	—	—	1	—
P.H. Edmonds	5	5	1	44	19	11.00	—	—	2	—
J.J. Whitaker	1	1	0	11	11	11.00	—	—	1	—
G.R. Dilley	4	4	2	6	4*	3.00	—	—	1	—

BOWLING

	O	M	R	W	A	BB	5I	10M
G.C. Small	78.4	23	180	12	15.00	5-48	2	—
G.R. Dilley	176.1	38	511	16	31.93	5-68	1	—
I.T. Botham	106.2	24	296	9	32.88	5-41	1	—
P.H. Edmonds	261.4	78	538	15	35.86	3-45	—	—
J.E. Emburey	315.5	86	663	18	36.83	7-78	2	—
P.A.J. DeFreitas	141.4	24	446	9	49.55	3-62	—	—
M.W. Gatting	23	7	39	0	—	—	—	—
A.J. Lamb	1	1	0	0	—	—	—	—

AUSTRALIA BATTING AND FIELDING

	M	I	NO	R	HS	A	100	50	ct	st
D.M. Jones	5	10	1	511	184*	56.77	1	3	1	—
G.R.J. Matthews	4	7	3	215	73*	53.75	—	2	6	—
A.R. Border	5	10	1	473	125	52.55	2	1	4	—
S.R. Waugh	5	8	1	310	79*	44.28	—	3	8	—
G.R. Marsh	5	10	0	429	110	42.90	1	2	5	—
G.M. Ritchie	4	8	2	244	46*	40.66	—	—	1	—
P.L. Taylor	1	2	0	53	42	26.50	—	—	—	—
D.C. Boon	4	8	0	144	103	18.00	1	—	1	—
T.J. Zoehrer	4	7	1	102	38	17.00	—	—	10	—
G.F. Lawson	1	1	0	13	13	13.00	—	—	1	—
D.M. Wellham	1	2	0	18	17	9.00	—	—	1	—
C.D. Matthews	2	3	0	21	11	7.00	—	—	1	—
P.R. Sleep	3	4	0	25	10	6.25	—	—	1	—
M.G. Hughes	4	6	0	31	16	5.16	—	—	2	—
B.A. Reid	5	7	4	14	4	4.66	—	—	—	—
C.J. McDermott	1	2	0	1	1	0.50	—	—	1	—
G.C. Dyer	1	—	—	—	—	—	—	—	2	—

BOWLING

	O	M	R	W	A	BB	5I	10M
P.L. Taylor	55	17	154	8	19.25	6-78	1	—
C.J. McDermott	26.5	4	83	4	20.75	4-83	—	—
B.A. Reid	198.4	44	527	20	26.35	4.64	—	—
P.R. Sleep	136	43	316	10	31.60	5-72	1	—
A.R. Border	16	6	32	1	32.00	1-25	—	—
S.R. Waugh	108.3	26	336	10	33.60	5-69	1	—
C.D. Matthews	70.1	14	233	6	38.83	3.95	—	—
M.G. Hughes	136.3	26	444	10	44.40	3-134	—	—
G.R.J. Matthews	83	11	295	2	147.50	1-10	—	—
G.F. Lawson	50	9	170	0	—	--	—	—

ENGLAND IN AUSTRALIA 1986–87 FINAL TOUR AVERAGES

BATTING AND FIELDING

	M	I	NO	R	HS	A	100	50	ct	st
N.A. Foster	4	6	2	172	74*	43.00	—	1	4	—
B.C. Broad	10	18	2	679	162	42.43	3	1	7	—
I.T. Botham	8	14	2	481	138	40.08	1	2	11	—
B.N. French	3	5	2	113	58	37.66	—	1	9	1
D.I. Gower	9	16	2	508	136	36.28	1	2	4	—
A.J. Lamb	10	18	1	534	105	31.41	1	3	11	—
J.J. Whitaker	5	7	0	214	108	30.57	1	—	2	—
M.W. Gatting	10	18	0	520	100	28.88	1	3	11	—
C.W.J. Athey	9	16	1	422	96	28.13	—	4	7	—
C.J. Richards	9	14	1	335	133	25.76	1	—	25	3
J.E. Emburey	9	14	3	279	69	25.36	—	1	6	—
W.N. Slack	5	9	0	184	89	20.44	—	1	5	—
P.A.J. DeFreitas	7	10	2	130	40	16.25	—	—	1	—
G.R. Dilley	6	6	3	39	32	13.00	—	—	1	—
G.C. Small	8	11	3	100	26	12.50	—	—	4	—
P.H. Edmonds	9	10	2	95	27	11.87	—	—	7	—

BOWLING

	O	M	R	W	A	BB	5I	10M
G.C. Small	258.4	72	626	33	18.96	5-48	3	—
M.W. Gatting	92	27	195	9	21.66	4-31	—	—
N.A. Foster	149	40	352	16	22.00	4-20	—	—
I.T. Botham	182.1	41	496	18	27.55	5-41	1	—
G.R. Dilley	231.1	44	685	21	32.61	5-68	1	—
J.E. Emburey	463.5	131	1023	31	33.00	7-78	3	—
P.A.J. DeFreitas	239	43	754	22	34.27	4-44	—	—
P.H. Edmonds	428.4	122	929	25	37.16	3-37	—	—
C.W.J. Athey	4	0	25	0	—	—	—	—
A.J. Lamb	1	1	0	0	—	—	—	—

TOUR SUMMARY

	played	won	lost	drawn
Test Matches	5	2	1	2
Other first-class	6	3	2	1
Perth Challenge	4	4	—	—
World Series Cup	10	6	4	—
Other matches	5	4	—	1
Total	30	19	7	4

GATTING – THIRD IN LINE

Mike Gatting is only the third England captain to retain the Ashes in Australia since the war. Len Hutton's team retained the Ashes won in 1953 on their 1954–55 tour, while Mike Brearley led his side to a convincing five-one victory in 1978–79. Ray Illingworth, whose side regained the Ashes in 1970–71, is the only other post-war captain to win a series in Australia.

In the 40 years since the Second World War Australia have held the Ashes for 23 of those years, England for only 17. But the Australian domination of Ashes contests between 1934 and 1953 and then between 1958–59 and 1970–71 has been matched by England's record since Illingworth's victory in 1970–71: they have held the Ashes for more than 11 out of the last 16 years, and now can look forward to keeping them until at least 1989.

POST-WAR TEST SERIES

Date	Venue	Played	Won by England	Won by Australia	Draw	Ashes held by
1946–47	Australia	5	0	3	2	Australia
1948	England	5	0	4	1	Australia
1950–51	Australia	5	1	4	0	Australia
1953	England	5	1	0	4	England
1954–55	Australia	5	3	1	1	England
1956	England	5	2	1	2	England
1958–59	Australia	5	0	4	1	Australia
1961	England	5	1	2	2	Australia
1962–63	Australia	5	1	1	3	Australia
1964	England	5	0	1	4	Australia
1965–66	Australia	5	1	1	3	Australia
1968	England	5	1	1	3	Australia
1970–71	Australia	6	2	0	4	England
1972	England	5	2	2	1	England
1974–75	Australia	6	1	4	1	Australia
1975	England	4	0	1	3	Australia
1976–77	Australia	1	0	1	0	✲
1977	England	5	3	0	2	England
1978–79	Australia	6	5	1	0	England
1979–80	Australia	3	0	3	0	✲
1980	England	1	0	0	1	✲
1981	England	6	3	1	2	England
1982–83	Australia	5	1	2	2	Australia
1985	England	6	3	1	2	England
1986–87	Australia	5	2	1	2	England

✲ The Ashes were not at stake in these matches.

		Played	Won by England	Won by Australia	Drawn	Series England	Series Australia
Totals	In England	57	16	14	27	5	4
	In Australia	62	17	26	19	4	6
		119	33	40	46	9	10

ONE-DAY CRICKET

The lowering of standards in the Australian Test side has been blamed on the number of one-day internationals played in recent seasons. In 1986–87 no fewer than 21 one-day internationals were contested in Australia. Australian teams played in a total of 19, six on their tour of India and 13 on home soil. World wide a total of 56 one-day internationals were arranged in the year between 1 September 1985 and 30 August 1986 and something like that number were due to be played by the end of August 1987.

England's staging of three or four matches in a home season, is a relatively modest contribution. But the emphasis on the 'one-dayer' Down Under has resulted in Australian players, some of them novices in Test cricket, playing huge numbers of one-day internationals. No wonder Allan Border sometimes finds it difficult to motivate himself: by the end of the 1986–87 World Series Cup he had represented his country 149 times in one-day matches, as well as playing 89 Tests. Steven Waugh, although only making his international début last winter, has played in 36 one-internationals, compared to 14 Tests. Likewise, Dean Jones has turned out for his country 45 times in one-day matches, only 10 times in Test matches. By contrast, Graham Gooch, an outstanding one-day player, played 'only' 48 one-day internationals between 1975 and 1986.

West Indies' one-day fortunes fluctuated dramatically in 1986–87. In Pakistan, they won four out of five one-day internationals and then won all three of their matches in Sharjah convincingly to capture the Champions Trophy. But, in Australia, they won only four out of 11 internationals, losing to Pakistan once, England four times and Australia twice. It was their batsmen rather than their bowlers who let them down as the final averages show.

England's one-day record in Australia was outstanding: they won ten out of 14 matches as they completed the second and third legs of their Grand Slam.

LEADING ONE-DAY AVERAGES IN AUSTRALIA 1986–87

BATTING

	M	I	NO	R	HS	Avge	100s	50s
Javed Miandad ...... (P)	4	4	1	196	77*	65.33	—	3
D.M. Jones ......(A)	13	13	0	623	121	47.92	3	2
A.J. Lamb......(E)	14	14	3	459	77*	41.72	—	3
B.C. Broad......(E)	14	14	0	559	97	39.92	—	5
Qasim Omar ......(P)	4	4	0	150	67	37.50	—	1
S.R. Waugh ......(A)	13	13	3	372	83*	37.20	—	2
I.V.A. Richards ......(WI)	11	10	0	334	70	33.40	—	3
G.R. Marsh ......(A)	13	13	0	415	94	31.92	—	2
A.R. Border ......(A)	13	13	1	370	91	30.83	—	2
I.T. Botham ......(E)	14	14	2	364	71	30.33	—	2
C.G. Greenidge ......(WI)	6	6	0	180	100	30.00	1	—
A.L. Logie ......(WI)	11	11	2	270	51	30.00	—	1
Shoaib Mohommad ......(P)	4	4	0	109	66	27.25	—	1
D.M. Wellham ......(A)	9	9	0	238	97	26.44	—	1
H.A. Gomes ......(WI)	6	6	0	155	43	25.83	—	—
C.W.J. Athey ......(E)	14	14	0	343	111	24.50	1	1
D.L. Haynes ......(WI)	9	9	0	217	67	24.11	—	1
S.P. O'Donnell ......(A)	13	12	5	161	52	23.00	—	1
P.J.L. Dujon ......(WI)	11	11	3	170	36	21.25	—	—
D.I. Gower ......(E)	14	14	0	291	50	20.78	—	1

LEADING ONE-DAY AVERAGES IN AUSTRALIA 1986–87

BOWLING

		O	M	R	W	A	BB	4W	R/O
Wasim Akram	(P)	37	6	126	8	15.75	3-27	—	3.40
G.R. Dilley	(E)	94.3	12	317	20	15.85	4-23	2	3.35
M.D. Marshall	(WI)	72.2	10	244	15	16.26	3-30	—	3.37
P.A.J. DeFreitas	(E)	121.1	14	391	21	18.61	4-35	1	3.22
A.H. Gray	(WI)	55.4	4	218	11	19.81	4-45	1	3.91
S.R. Waugh	(A)	109.5	4	458	21	21.80	4-48	1	4.17
G.R.J. Matthews	(A)	91.1	7	313	14	22.35	3-27	—	3.43
J. Garner	(WI)	87	7	324	14	23.14	5-47	1	3.72
J.E. Emburey	(E)	127.5	3	578	22	26.27	4-37	1	4.52
S.P. O'Donnell	(A)	111	6	506	19	26.63	4-19	2	4.55
C.A. Walsh	(WI)	97.1	8	360	13	27.69	3-46	—	3.70
P.L. Taylor	(A)	82.1	4	337	12	28.08	3-29	—	4.10
R.A. Harper	(WI)	105	2	425	13	32.69	3-49	—	4.04

FIELDING

WICKET-KEEPERS

DISMISSALS			
17	(16ct, 1st)	T.J. Zoehrer	(A)
13	(11ct, 2st)	P.J.L. Dujon	(WI)
10	(9ct, 1st)	C.J. Richards	(E)
6	(5ct, 1st)	B.N. French	(E)
	(6ct)	Salim Yousuf	(P)

OUTFIELDERS

CATCHES		
10	C.W.J. Athey	(E)
9	J. Garner	(WI)
8	R.A. Harper	(WI)
	J.E. Emburey	(E)
7	D.I. Gower	(E)
6	A.R. Border	(A)
	P.A.J. DeFreitas	(E)
	G.R.J. Matthews	(A)
	I.V.A. Richards	(WI)
	R.B. Richardson	(WI)
	D.M. Wellham	(A)
5	M.W. Gatting	(E)
	S.P. O'Donnell	(A)
	P.L. Taylor	(A)